MW00324587

PRAISE FOR

From Hot Mess to God's Best

Our brains are more complex than any supercomputer. Through it, we experience emotions like love and joy while involuntary actions naturally occur like breathing and beating hearts. Computers were created by the human race but man and woman were created by God. The most impressive quality of the human mind is the ability to have a relationship with the One True God through His Son, Jesus Christ. "From Hot Mess to God's Best" is a home run for those looking to embrace being created in God's image and taking practical steps to declutter your mind as you run towards glorifying God in all you do.

—**Miguel R. Viera**, author, *Mission Minded in the Workplace: Illuminating the fruit of the Spirit*

***

From Hot Mess to God's Best: Decluttering Your Mess to Be Your Best is a witty, helpful book that helps increase awareness of areas in our lives that are messy and provides strategies for decluttering our minds. In addition, it provides us with ideas and strategies so that we can start living out God's best for our lives.

The book made me realize that I was still a hot mess even though I thought I'd conquered these things long ago! And it helped me work on fixing them. If you're ready to stop being such a hot mess, read this book!

—**Emerald Barnes**, author of the *Entertaining Angels* series

***

Leslie Spea's *From Hot Mess to God's Best: Decluttering Your Mess to Be Your Best* combats some of the most relatable worldly struggles with the truth of God's Word. This book is perfect for people in all walks of life and in all stages of their relationship with God as it is both honest and encouraging. These pages are full of practical, biblical tools to help anyone in their journey to rid their minds of lies from the enemy and make their life better reflect Christ's!

—**Bailey Lynn**, author of *Unforseen* baileylynnbooks.com

***

From Hot Mess to God's Best is a timely must-read as we face such challenging times. Leslie's book is thought-provoking and sprinkled with humor. I love how Leslie uses Bible verses throughout to encourage the reader to be introspective and choose to improve. Her use of humor is refreshing. I encourage you to read this book.

—**Wendy R. Randall**, author of *Once there was a girl*

From Hot Mess to God's Best

Decluttering Your Mess to Be Your Best

LESLIE SPEAS

Published by KHARIS PUBLISHING, imprint of KHARIS MEDIA LLC.

Copyright © 2022 Leslie Speas

ISBN-13: 978-1-63746-159-4
ISBN-10: 1-63746-159-3

Library of Congress Control Number: 2022942608

All KHARIS PUBLISHING products are available at special quantity discounts for bulk purchase for sales promotions, premiums, fund-raising, and educational needs. For details, contact:

Kharis Media LLC
Tel: 1-479-599-8657
support@kharispublishing.com
www.kharispublishing.com

Table of Contents

Introduction

Decluttering Your Mess

Are you a hot mess? Or maybe just a warm or smoldering mess? Although we don't like to admit it, I think we all have our hot mess moments. So, exactly what is a hot mess? Urban Dictionary's definition is *when someone's thoughts or appearance are in a state of disarray, but they maintain an undeniable attractiveness*. Really what it boils down to is someone who doesn't have their sh*# together.

I self-identify as a hot mess and am probably not a typical Christian author. I compare. I try to control. I'm often stressed and anxious. I have a crazy mind. I really like wine. My sense of humor is off-color. But I sure love Jesus and honestly don't know how I would have survived the last few years without my faith. I have felt a continued nudge to share my issues through writing so here I go with my second book about being a hot mess. I'm not sure how many it will take!

Are we born with this mess? I don't think so. I believe we accumulate it as we walk through life, a little more each day. Our earthly disappointments and experiences impact who we become.

We try to protect ourselves out of fear and shame and this limits our potential. We try to avoid rejection. We try to find our worth through pleasing others. We try to achieve success according to the world's standards. By the time we get to fifty-something, unless we declutter regularly, we have likely accumulated a mountain of mess. This mess gets in our way and holds us back from doing things we were meant to do and being who we were meant to be.

I don't know about you, but a cluttery, messy space stresses me out. In my house, I do a rather good job of decluttering. Every time my family can't find something, I am typically to blame. My stepdaughter still brings up a Scooby-Doo that I took to Goodwill over ten years ago.

My husband likes to keep everything. One of the many ways that we are opposites. Until recently, he had his books and notes from college thirty-plus years ago. And they were mostly about Wood Science, a major he has never used. I try not to declutter his stuff as he is very protective, but boy do I want to!

Unfortunately, I am not as good at decluttering other things in my life as I am around the house. In fact, I could be on an episode of Hoarders for all the issues that I have accumulated over the years that don't add value.

Have you ever seen Hot Mess House on HGTV? Four organizing types are shared on this show. I am a ladybug which means I can shove everything into a cabinet or closet and be okay with it. I just don't like it in my line of sight. Pretty much how I have lived my life until recently. I generally kept my mess inside and looked okay on the outside. Now the mess has exceeded the space and is coming out of the closet! At this point, I am ready to embark on the journey of decluttering my closets and decluttering my mind.

In this book, we will be exploring issues that many of us have accumulated in our lives including comparison, control, guilt, people-pleasing, fear, disappointment, and more. These issues can result in strongholds which are mindsets or attitudes that typically negatively impact our lives.

I love acronyms and have created this one to describe what I would like to achieve as a result of this book.

H – Helping
O – Others
T – To
M – Make
E – Every
S – Stronghold
S – Scarce

It sums up my goal - to help others declutter the issues that are holding them back from their best lives. Can we declutter all of our issues at one time? Probably not, we are human and will always struggle but it is possible to go from a hot mess to progress, chipping away at one area at a time by turning to God and by using the information shared. So, let's get started!

Chapter One

Scrapping Your Strongholds

The mind is undoubtedly an amazing thing. It is extremely complex. It is often disobedient. It is all over the place. It feels uncontrollable at times – in fact, much of the time for me. My mind goes a thousand miles a minute and often to places where it is not good for it to go. I just saw a post on Facebook that said, *My mind is like an internet browser. 17 tabs are open, 4 of them are frozen and I don't know where the music is coming from*. In my case, that's about right! Most, if not all, of our mess, originates in our minds. In this chapter, we will further explore the mind and the strongholds that can develop.

I have often wished that I had the mind of a dog. Have you ever seen the meme where a guy is sitting beside a dog looking over a pond? The guy has a bubble over his head with pictures of numerous things that are running through it. I bet there would be even more if he were female! The dog just has a picture of the pond in his bubble. I cannot say 100% what goes through a dog's mind, but I would bet that it is simpler, and more in the moment than what goes through the human mind.

I remember hiking with my husband one day. I asked him what he was thinking about. He replied, "I'm thinking about where I am going to put my pole next." I had already done a review of the last few years, worried about my kids' futures, and planned our next vacation and we were only twenty minutes in. So, I guess he may think kind of like a dog, but most of us don't. He also says that he doesn't dream while I have crazy, jacked-up dreams. My mind is still going even when I'm sleeping. I dreamed about a talking skunk and platypuses running around in my backyard the other night. Analyze that!

Our thoughts pretty much control our lives. Henry Ford said, *"Whether you think you can or think you can't, you're right."* Until I started researching the topic and praying about it, I thought that there was nothing that could be done to control the mind. Thankfully, I discovered that it is possible to learn how to guard it, strengthen it, and renew it.

The Apostle Paul challenges us to *"not conform to the pattern of this world but be transformed by the renewing of our minds"* (Romans 12:1-2). The Greek word for renew is *anakainosis* and it means renovation. We have recently been doing some renovations to update and upgrade our home. I can tell you that my mind needs an "extreme home makeover." I have made progress but still need serious work. What kind of renovation does your mind need – extreme or just a few upgrades?

Our minds are the first thing that Satan goes after. Paul says, *"For though we live in the world, we do not wage war as the world does. The weapons we fight with are not the weapons of the world. On the contrary, they have divine power to demolish strongholds. We demolish arguments and every pretension that sets itself up against the knowledge of God, and we take captive every thought to make it obedient to Christ"* (2 Corinthians 10:3-5).

Paul mentioned strongholds. What are strongholds? Dictionary.com defines a stronghold as *a place where a particular cause or belief is strongly defended or upheld.* In short, it is a mindset or attitude. There are many strongholds that we may experience including comparison, fear, guilt, pride, materialism, and more.

We aren't born with these strongholds. We accumulate them through our life events and experiences, and Satan's deceitful guidance. Strongholds are often manifested as damaged thought patterns that play like a broken record in our minds. For example, let's say that a close friend or family member deeply betrayed your trust and hurt you. The enemy then whispers that you cannot trust anyone, so you develop trust issues which then result in an unwillingness to trust God's promises in your life.

Second Corinthians 4:4 says, *"The god of this age [a reference to Satan and his demons] has blinded the minds of unbelievers so that they cannot see the light of the gospel that displays the glory of Christ, who is the image of God."* If this is his approach for those that aren't Christians, it stands to reason that his strategy in the lives of Christians is to confuse, frustrate, and separate us from God. And he does this largely through strongholds.

If you aren't sure what strongholds might be affecting your life, here are three questions to ask yourself to get to the root of them. *What is a constant battleground in my life? What unhealthy habit or unhealthy thought pattern has a hold on me? What do I constantly struggle with?*

At the foundation of many of our strongholds is a desire to want to prove our significance and value, often because we don't feel that we're worthy of love, acceptance, or success. However, we must acknowledge that our value is not determined by whether people like us or not, nor is it determined by our performance or worldly success. It is established by who we are in Christ.

Paul gives us the formula to test our thoughts. In Philippians 4:8, he tells us to think about things that are *true, noble, right, pure, lovely, admirable, excellent, and worthy of praise.* I like the Message's translation of this, it tells us *to fill our minds with the best, not the worst; the beautiful, not the ugly; things to praise, not things to curse.*

What can you do to renew and declutter your messy mind? Here are five general tips. More specific tips on each stronghold will be shared in the respective chapters.

1. **Foster awareness and acknowledgment of your strongholds**

   As with any issue we may face, the first step to recovery is awareness and acknowledgment of the problem, and a desire to truly change. Ask God to show you your strongholds and the resulting negative thought patterns that exist in your life. Pray the following Psalms:

   Psalm 69:5: *You God, know my folly; my guilt is not hidden from thee.*

   Psalm 19:12: *But who can discern their errors? Forgive my hidden faults.*

   When He reveals or confirms these negative patterns, don't shift the blame to others. Ask God to forgive you for believing the lies that have created your strongholds and for reacting in ungodly ways.

2. **Fill your mind with good stuff and take out the bad stuff**

   As was mentioned, Paul tells us to *"renew our minds"* and we can do that through a steady intake of God's Word. In 1

Peter 2:2, Peter calls Christians to *"crave the spiritual milk so that by it you may grow up in your salvation."* Think about the things that you are filling your mind with – television, social media, the news, books, etc. Have you ever heard the term, garbage in garbage out? That's how it works with our minds. If you fill it with garbage, the result will be garbage. For some reason, this is bringing up images of Oscar the Grouch. As I've said, crazy mind.

Proverbs 15:14 says, *"The discerning heart seeks knowledge but the mouth of a fool feeds on folly."* We should read our Bibles and fill our minds with knowledge and positive things. I'm a fine example! Earlier this evening, I was watching *The Bachelorette* while scrolling through social media, but at least I am acknowledging the problem.

3. **Recognize and reject Satan's lies**

We have maintained that Satan tempts and troubles us by putting ideas and thoughts in our minds. He does this by preying on our struggles and past hurts. Let's just call this what it is – lies. Recognize and reject his lies and replace them with God's truth (look for passages to support His truth). I know my thoughts are often coming from a place of feeling like I'm not good enough. And I now have my go-to Bible verses to help me overcome this narrative.

In 2 Corinthians 10:5, we are told to take captive every thought to make it obedient to Christ. This indicates that we actually have the power to do something about it. If I have an ungodly thought, I try to redirect myself and say, *"get away Satan."* I then ask God for the strength to help me overcome. Helpful tip - you may want to say *"get away Satan"* to yourself or it may generate unwanted attention. But, if you do it in Walmart, no one will notice, too many other distractions.

In Romans 7:19, Paul says *"For I do not do the good I want to do, but the evil I do not want to do – this I keep on doing."* I feel you, Paul. The struggle is real! But we can begin to make progress, one thought at a time.

4. Overcome the negative narratives that are guiding your life

In the book, *Enough: Silencing the Lies That Steal Your Confidence,*[1] Sharon Jaynes suggests trying to recognize I AM NOT thoughts and speech and switch them with I AM. When you say, "I AM NOT smart enough," mentally change this to "I AM" smart enough." Sharon suggests "spotting the nots" in your life, swatting them out of your mind, and replacing them with the truth.

5. Focus on the good things/blessings around you

Have you ever noticed that people tend to focus on the negative? This is called the negativity bias and we, as humans, are wired that way. This bias is hardwired into our human nature and is designed to protect us. In ancient times, our ancestors were frequently exposed to threats like predators, and being more attentive to negative stimuli helped them survive. Since our world has evolved, we aren't frequently faced with imminent danger like being chased by lions, tigers, and bears. Although who knows with the way the world has been going the last few years!

That said, it is important to shift your mind towards gratitude for things like eyes to see, ears to hear, family,

---

[1] Sharon Jaynes, *Enough: Silencing the Lies That Steal Your Confidence* (Eugene, Oregon: Harvest House Publishers, 2018).

friends, a place to live, and the beauty of nature. Keeping a gratitude journal and recording things that you are thankful for each day can be helpful. Lately, I have taken to identifying five things in the morning that I am grateful for and five additional things before I go to bed. I have observed that coffee and my dogs come up a lot, especially in the morning. Occasionally, my husband and kids make the list.

In conclusion, strongholds are frequently the root of many of the issues that we need to declutter from our lives. We will be exploring twelve of the most common strongholds in this book and provide some specific suggestions that hopefully will help you to conquer them.

NOT ENOUGH

DISAPPOINTMENT

COMPARISON & JEALOUSY

UNHEALTHY MINDSETS

CONTROL

HOT MESS MIND

THE 2 P'S

ANGER & BITTERNESS

GUILT & SHAME

PRIDE

FEARSOME FOURSOME

REJECTION

WORLDLY FOCUS

Chapter Two

Flushing Feeling Like You Aren't Enough

(Stronghold Number One)

But because of his great love for us, God, who is rich in mercy, made us alive with Christ even when we were dead in transgressions—it is by grace you have been saved. And God raised us with Christ and seated us with him in the heavenly realms in Christ Jesus. —Ephesians 2:4-6

One of my biggest strongholds is feeling like I'm not good enough. This underlying pervasive, thought pattern goes through my head frequently and negatively impacts my life. I believe this is a stronghold for many of us, especially women.

So, where does this feeling come from? It is inevitable that the environment and experiences of our childhood affect us and how we feel about ourselves. Maybe you grew up in an unstable or broken home. Or you were picked on as a child because you were overweight or uncool. Kids can be mean and bullying and teasing can have a lasting impact. I'm still scarred because a guy in junior high said that I looked like a mon chi chi (google it). I was also told that I looked like Linda Blair in the Exorcist and worried about whether it was before or after her head spun around and she had projectile vomit. I digress, which you will see happens fairly often.

Some of us have more sensitive personalities and this may contribute to how we feel about ourselves. And sometimes trauma and other difficult experiences later in life can leave us feeling that we aren't good enough. I am not sure where this narrative came from in my case. Part of it may stem from my parents' divorce where, although it didn't have anything to do with me, I believed at some level that I was partially at fault. Later, I was in an emotionally abusive relationship that confirmed in my head that I wasn't good enough.

Until I read a few books on the subject, I had never really thought about the story I was telling myself. Some examples which have plagued me over the years and may be plaguing some of you are below:

I'm not enough!
I'm not strong enough.
I'm not smart enough.
I'm not brave enough.
I'm not talented enough.
I'm not a good enough mother/spouse/friend/employee.
I'm not thin enough.
I'm not pretty enough.
I'm not domestic enough (okay, this one is true for me - I'm about as domestic as a cardboard box).

So many people say or do unkind things to us in this world. We should be kind and speak to ourselves as we would a friend. Proverbs 18:21 says, *"the tongue has the power of life or death"*, and that includes how we talk to ourselves!

So, what is good enough anyway? Good enough for what? For whom? What would you need to achieve to be enough? What would you have to do or be to be enough? You can probably list several ideas: *"I'd be good enough if I...didn't snap at my kids, made more money, lost twenty pounds, spent time with God every day, stopped procrastinating..."* But these examples are nebulous. How many things would you need to change to be enough? If you think about it, this involves seeking approval from something that only exists in your mind and will never be satisfied. You could spend your whole life trying to achieve, be, and do the right things to show your worth to the world and still not feel like you are good enough.

Many of us suffer from negative thinking that is rooted in this stronghold. Here's a personal example: I have been upset about my daughter. Why? Because she has experienced hardships over the past few years. Why is that bad? I want her to have a good life and be happy and successful. What does that mean? I'm not a good enough parent and am at fault for her problems.

Feeling not good enough results in feelings of insecurity. So, we will expand on this topic a bit. Insecurity is defined as a *significant lack of self-confidence, a strong fear of others' disapproval or rejection, or a chronic sense of inferiority.* It involves a deep sense of doubt about your worth and place in the world. Insecurity comes in many different shapes and forms. Some people are insecure about their bodies, meanwhile, others are insecure about their work, upbringing, possessions, intelligence, looks, social skills, etc. Insecurity makes us feel that we don't measure up.

I guess feelings of insecurity probably start early in life as toddlers use pacifiers and blankets to feel more secure. I had a baby pillow and a stuffed dog named Droopy when I was little. I slept with Droopy until college and he was pretty much threadbare, and I still sleep with a baby pillow to this day. My childhood friend was so attached to her blanket that her mom made a coat out of it when she got older. And my brother loved his pacifier which he called "pu" and didn't want to give it up until way past the normal age. But I digress again...The point is that insecurity starts early in life.

Whether we are aware of it or not, our insecurities often seep into our relationships and impact our behavior. We have maintained that Satan is the father of lies and it's one of his favorite tactics to hold God's children hostage to a life that is "less than." He tells us insidious lies so that we will focus on our flaws rather than on our faith.

Feeling not enough and insecure isn't a new problem. When God called Moses to lead His people out of Egyptian bondage, Moses had a big case of the "not-good-enoughs." An argument with God ensued where Moses said he wasn't brave enough, strong enough, smart enough, eloquent enough, charismatic enough, or confident enough. (Exodus 3:10-16)

In Judges 6, Gideon was called to lead the Israelites out of captivity. Gideon claimed he was from a weak clan and the least in his family. Check out what he says in Judges 6:14-15:

> The LORD turned to him and said, "Go in the strength you have and save Israel out of Midian's hand. Am I not sending you?" "Pardon me, my lord," Gideon replied, "but how can I save Israel? My clan is the weakest in Manasseh, and I am the least in my family."

Certainly, as I felt called to share my struggles through writing, I questioned God. *"Are you sure? I'm kind of a mess! There are so many reasons why I'm not your girl. What could I possibly share with others that would help bring them closer to you?"* I am very hesitant to compare myself to Moses or Gideon but sort of the same idea. Feeling not good enough!

We all have voices in our heads that come from other people - a disapproving parent, a boss, a teacher, or even ourselves. In Gideon's case, insecurity caused him to ask God for not just one, but two, miraculous signs to strengthen his faith. (Judges 6:36-40) This part of Gideon's story shows us that mastering our insecurities doesn't happen in a moment. We will likely have successes and failures. But through it all, God is patient and kind.

So, what can we do to be good enough? Well, here's some news that will alleviate some of the pressure. None of us is good enough without the help of Christ. We were created to depend on Him for everything. Alone, we are sinful people who are capable of nothing good. Christ is the one who makes us enough! We don't have to try to be enough because He has that covered for us.

Here are a few things that you can do to declutter this stronghold from your life.

1. Affirm your worth by reading scripture that confirms how God sees you. When you recognize a false belief about your worth, reject it, and replace it with these truths.

    -   I am deeply and completely loved (Romans 8:38-39)
    -   I am fearfully and wonderfully made (Psalm 139:14)
    -   I am holy and dearly loved (Colossians 3:12)
    -   I am free from condemnation (Romans 8:1)
    -   I am totally and completely forgiven (1 John 2:12)

- I mean the world to Him (John 3:16)
- He thinks I am beautiful right now (Song of Solomon 4:1)
- When God sees me, He sees the righteousness of Jesus (2 Corinthians 5:21)

2. Recognize that God made you for a purpose and that includes your talents, body, quirks, weaknesses, and passions. You are the only one alive who was or ever will be you. I am personally trying to grow in believing that I am completely loved at the moment and that God isn't waiting for me to get my act together. He knows everything about me and loves me anyway.

Starting now, I am going to flush the feeling that I am not enough and focus on the reality that I am enough because of Jesus' power and presence in me. If this is a stronghold for you, I hope you will do the same!

Chapter Three

Clearing Out Comparison and Junking Jealousy

(Stronghold Number Two)

Each one should test his actions. Then they can take pride in themselves alone, without comparing themselves to somebody else. —Galatians 6:4

Comparison and the jealousy that will likely result are strongholds that affect many of us. For as long as I can remember, I have compared myself to others. Since I'm a hot mess, this doesn't always go well. I don't know when comparison starts to rear its ugly head, but I believe that it's pretty darn early in our lives.

As a little girl, I wanted blond hair and cute ponytails like Cindy Brady on *The Brady Bunch* television show. I had a childhood friend that was from a wealthy family. She had a speaker system and an indoor pool in her house – and a really cool dollhouse. I was envious and wondered why she had all the neat stuff, and I didn't. As I got a little older, I remember comparing myself to other girls and thinking that they were smarter, prettier, more athletic, and more popular and wishing that I could be more like them. I think I peaked in fourth grade when I was voted Safety Patrol of the Year, and everyone wanted to be my friend. It didn't last very long though. My youngest daughter said she peaked in preschool when she had everyone in her class running around on all fours like dogs. I think she might have been the preschool mean girl.

The comparison problem persisted for me up through high school, college, and into adulthood, although the things that I compare have shifted over time. I no longer covet blond ponytails and a speaker system (those are a little obsolete as my husband now talks to me through the doorbell when he isn't even home). At this point in my life, I'm most likely to feel pangs of jealousy related to job achievements, material possessions, cool vacations, and families that seem to have it all together. Mine does not.

We compare ourselves in so many ways. Our intelligence. Our parenting. Our bodies. Our looks. Our achievements. Our marital status. Our material possessions. Our careers. We all have unique gifts and talents. If we compare ourselves in areas that are not in line with these gifts and talents, it's not likely to go well. I am a terrible cook and am known for bringing chips and dip (store-bought) to gatherings. People encourage me NOT to cook. I am also no good at gardening. I have a brown thumb and can make plants die by walking by. It is my superpower. If I compare myself with friends who are "Martha Stewarty" (and I have a few), I am sunk.

Even in our areas of talent, there is always likely to be someone better. If we are at the top of our game. It won't last forever. So, we should focus on doing our best and forgetting the rest. I think I got that saying from the P90X guy but I like it.

Social media has undeniably dramatically increased the information about others that we are exposed to, thus fueling the fire of social comparison. Now the Joneses are in our faces all the time. It just takes a scroll to see an update that makes us feel envious or like our life pales in comparison. But we have to keep in mind that social media usually only shows the picture of others' lives that they want us to see. They got some mess too ya'll, even if it doesn't show in their public personas.

Back in the day, there was no social media or Smart Phones. We didn't know what was going on in the lives of others unless we heard it through the grapevine, maintained contact by phone, wrote letters, or actually saw someone. I know that is hard for young people to believe but somehow, we survived. And we had to walk uphill in the snow to school for five miles (not really). However, my generation will have some great 2020/2021 stories to share with our grandchildren!

I feel for kids growing up today as I am sure social media further amplifies the insecurities that are typically experienced during those years. I have observed the effect on my kids who are now in their twenties, and it hasn't been positive.

So, why are we prone to making comparisons? Comparison is a fundamental human impulse and there isn't any way to shut it down completely. In some ways, comparing yourself to others can be helpful. You may feel inspired by someone else's achievement which may motivate you to improve your own life. Or you may recognize that your abilities are a notch above someone else's which may boost your self-esteem. But as a caveat, you have to be careful as this is a slippery slope that may lead to pride. With a few exceptions, I think that comparing ourselves to others makes us feel that we are chronically inferior or just generally don't measure up.

Back to my wish that my brain was more like a dog's. Do dogs think, "I wish I was tall and thin like that Great Dane" or, "I wish my nose looked like a Pug" or, "I think that Poodle is smarter than me?" I don't think they spend time wishing they were something that they aren't. They just accept themselves, and focus on things like eating, playing, and sleeping. Must be nice!

Making comparisons is certainly nothing new, and it rarely ends well. Cain compared himself to Abel. Jesus' disciples struggled with comparison by trying to determine which of them would suffer in the future, and who would be spared. (John 21:23)

A classic example of comparison gone wrong is the story of Rachel and Lea in Genesis. It reads a lot like a soap opera. Jacob fell in love with Rachel and worked for her father, Laban, for seven years to win her hand in marriage. Laban conspired against Jacob to hand Leah (his older, weak-eyed daughter) over in marriage instead. Not sure what weak-eyed means exactly but thinking she was the one with the "good personality." So, Jacob ends up marrying Rachel as well but had to serve Laban another seven years.

Genesis 29 tells us that Jacob loved Rachel more than Leah. When the Lord saw this, he opened Leah's womb and she gave birth to four sons. When Rachel observed that she was not bearing Jacob any children, she became jealous of Leah. (Genesis 30:1) And so, the battle began. Since she wasn't having success conceiving, Rachel had two children through her maidservant and finally had a child on her own. God then helped Rachel conceive again but this time there was less celebration. It resulted in her death.

The situation between Leah and Rachel created a bunch of drama. Although Rachel was beautiful and had the love of her husband, she didn't enjoy her life as she was always comparing herself with her sister. She pushed away a relationship that could have been a blessing, ultimately ending up alone.

As in this case, comparing ourselves to others usually results in jealousy. We want what others have. We desire to look like them. We desire to live like them. We desire to be like them. We can't focus on what God's asking us to do because we want to be doing what they're doing.

The word "jealously" in Webster's dictionary is defined as *zealous vigilance*. The Bible says in Proverbs 27:4, *"Anger is cruel and fury overwhelming, but who can stand before jealousy?"* Jealousy is probably one of the world's oldest emotions. Back to the story of Cain and Abel, the sons of Adam and Eve, the Lord looked more favorably on Abel's offering than on Cain's. Cain became jealous and killed Abel. Now there's a prime example of jealousy run amok!

Another example of how destructive jealously can be is the story of Joseph and his brothers. Joseph was his father's favorite. His father gave him a coat of many colors which was an indicator of Joseph's favor in his eyes. This ticked his brothers off. Then, Joseph shared a dream he had with them that said that he would rule over them someday. Now, they were really angry and jealous of Joseph. As a result, they threw him into a pit and sold him into slavery.

In Scripture, God is often described as a jealous God. (Exodus 20:5, Deuteronomy 4:23, Zechariah 8:2) Exodus 34:12-14 says, *"Be careful not to make a treaty with those who live in the land where you are going, or they will be a snare among you. Break down their altars, smash their sacred stones, and cut down their Asherah poles. Do not worship any other god, for the Lord, whose name is Jealous, is a jealous God."*

You may ask yourself, *"If God can be jealous, then I can too, right?"* The answer is no because it is quite different. God's jealousy is always a product of his perfect, self-sufficient love (Exodus 3:14, Psalm 50:9-15, Isaiah 40:28), which enables Him to feel deeply jealous about the people which He created, especially when we put other idols in front of him. Humans, in contrast, are usually jealous as a product of our finite love, insecurity, entitlement, and unmet expectations.

The Bible has a lot to say about jealousy. Here are a few Scriptures on the topic that spoke to me.

> *For where you have envy and selfish ambition, there you find disorder and every evil practice.* —James 3:16

> *A heart at peace gives life to the body, but envy rots the bones.* — Proverbs 14:30

> *You desire but do not have, so you kill. You covet but you cannot get what you want, so you quarrel and fight. You do not have it because you do not ask God. When you ask, you do not receive, because you ask with wrong motives, that you may spend what you get on your pleasures.* —James 4: 2-3

How can we overcome our tendency towards comparison and the jealousy which will likely result? I am still working on that. I think that, to some extent, it is something that we will never overcome entirely while we are in this world, but we can certainly go from hot mess to progress!

Here are three decluttering strategies that you can use to clear out the comparison and junk the resulting jealousy:

1. **Start noticing the triggers that cause you to play the comparison game**

   Identify the activities or circumstances that make you feel discontent about your life. Maybe you drive through a neighborhood frequently that makes you wish you had a bigger, nicer house. Stop doing that! Or maybe you have a friend that is often bragging about her material possessions or her kids. Distance yourself!

   To identify your triggers, ask yourself questions like:

   1. *What books or magazines do I need to stop reading?*
   2. *What social media accounts or people do I need to stop following?*
   3. *What TV shows do I need to stop watching?*
   4. *Are there any places where I need to stop going?*
   5. *Are there any people I need to spend less time around?*

2. **Remind yourself that you can't use a person's outward appearance to judge the reality of their life**

   People carefully craft the social media and public versions of themselves to look like they have much more together than they do in reality. Everyone is fighting battles that we know nothing about, and most people don't put it out there on social media. Unless they are a hot mess that feels called to do so like me!

3. **Remember that the Bible says to love your neighbor**

   We can't love people well when we're too busy trying to measure our value by them or prove that we are superior. First Corinthians 13 says, *"love rejoices with others."* If we love others, we don't become jealous or resentful when they succeed. If a coworker gets a promotion, or a friend loses weight and looks great, instead of succumbing to comparison, compliment them! Genuinely complimenting others outwardly keeps us from complaining inwardly.

Comparison and jealousy breed discontentment in our lives and steal our joy. The reason we compare ourselves is that deep inside we are dissatisfied with what we have and who we are. But God has uniquely and precisely created us with specific gifts and talents to do what He's called us to do. Ephesians 2:10 tells us, *"For we are God's handiwork, created in Christ Jesus to do good works, which God prepared in advance for us to do."* Who are we to question His plan for us? So, let's clear out comparison and junk any resulting jealousy so that we can be who He made us be and use our gifts and talents to make the world a better place.

Chapter Four

Cleaning Up Control

(Stronghold Number Three)

"If you want to make God laugh, tell Him about your plans." —Woody Allen

Do you like the feeling of being in control? I sure do. I MAY be a bit of a control freak. I love to have my plans and feel like I can dictate how things will go. It baffles me that others don't follow my plans because we would all be so much better off!

I have come to realize that I'm rarely, if ever, in control of what happens. The pandemic that we are experiencing as I write this is proof of that. We may have control over our actions, attitudes, and responses, but that is about it. God is in control of everything else. Although I am very aware of this, when something happens that concerns me, I still get in there and try to set things straight. I guess this means that I secretly think that I'm in control and don't trust God to handle it.

So, what exactly is control? Control is defined as *the power to direct people's behavior or the course of events*. *"I like being controlled,"* said …No one. Ever. Controlling can be very damaging to relationships. And often it is the people closest to us that we try to control. Controlling behavior can be motivated by love, initially with good intentions, but it seldom turns out well.

When we come into this world, we are dependent on our parents or guardians for everything. As we get older and start to accumulate mess, we often feel that we have to take control of circumstances and people in our lives to stay safe or have the best outcome. In reality, we should revert to where we were as infants and trust God to handle things for us. It would make our lives a whole lot easier!

There were undoubtedly some skeptical, control freaks in the Bible. Let's explore the story of Sarah and Abraham in Genesis 16. The Lord told Abraham and Sarah that they would bear a child. Sarah got tired of waiting so she took control of the situation and pressured Abraham into having a baby with her maidservant, Hagar. This wasn't the best idea as Sarah came to resent Hagar. Sarah eventually had a child of her own and lots of drama ensued. By the way, I don't understand the whole having babies with the maidservants' thing. Seems like a recipe for disaster.

Rebekah in Genesis 27 provides us with another example of controlling behavior. Rebekah overheard her husband's plan to bless their oldest son, Esau. She then took matters into her own hands to make sure that her younger (and favorite) son, Jacob, was blessed instead. She forced her plan instead of asking for God's will to prevail. And guess what? The result was not good. Jacob ended up fearing for his life and running away as a result.

We are all too familiar with the story of Adam and Eve where Eve manipulated and tried to control Adam by encouraging him to eat the apple. Manipulate is a pretty strong word to use for controlling behavior, isn't it? It often has a negative and demeaning connotation, suggesting intentional, malicious action. Sometimes manipulation may be desperation for an outcome or behavior that causes us to step over boundaries and try to influence the situation or person. When I think of this word, I think, *"I don't do that, do I?"* If I am honest with myself, I have probably done this quite a lot over the years.

So, how else has controlling behavior manifested itself in my life? When I was married the first time, I thought I could change my husband, so I tried to control and manipulate him to some extent. This didn't work well as he too was a control freak. Probably a part of the reason that it was my first marriage! Tip for you younger women out there; don't go into a relationship thinking you can change the other person. Only God can do that.

My biggest struggle with control has been in my role as a mother. When my kids were small, I had a great deal of control over their lives. I was able to direct what they did, who they hung out with, what they ate, and how they behaved. And I even got to pick out what they wore. My youngest let me do this until middle school. Much to my chagrin, in seventh grade, she went into an emo phase. Not sure what that means but I think it's a modified version of Goth. Since then, she has had every color of hair, multiple piercings, tattoos, etc. Not what I envisioned but, of course, I love her very much and respect her individuality. My other daughter wears sweats all the time with Birkenstocks – and her feet are not open-toed-shoe ready! Okay, so I'm probably a little overly concerned with appearance but just can't seem to help myself.

Now that my children are in their twenties, any semblance of control has diminished. They are on the cusp of making so many decisions that will impact their lives long-term – what career to choose, how they take care of their health, who to have a relationship with or marry to name a few - and they rarely listen to me anymore. I have overstepped boundaries at times. I know at a conscious level that I can't control their lives, but I still attempt to sometimes. I guess I am trying to steer them towards my plan which apparently doesn't line up with God's plan for their lives. I know His plan is much better but still push for mine!

Proverbs 19:21 says, *"Many are the plans in a person's heart, but it is the Lord's purpose that prevails."* Even knowing this, it's hard to overcome the desire to control people and events to make them go the way we think they should.

Here are four strategies that can help you clean up control if you struggle with it as I do.

1. Awareness is important

Understanding what is within your control, and what is not, is critical. You have control over your thoughts, feelings, and behaviors. However, you are not in control of others' thoughts, feelings, and actions. This does not mean you shouldn't be concerned about them but you should release the idea or any attempts to control others or circumstances to God.

2. Understand the why

When you understand why we are attempting to control, you can effectively address the heart of the problem. You can do this by journaling or pondering the following:

- *Identify a time when you were controlling.*
- *What happened?*
- *How did you feel or respond?*
- *What were you afraid would happen if you didn't intervene?*

- *How could you have responded without trying to control it?*
- *What will you do differently in the future?*

For me, I think the "why" for my desire to control my children is rooted in a fear that they will not be financially independent, mentally healthy, or happy. And, if I'm honest, I think a little of it is based on me trying to live out what I wished I might have been or done through them. And some of it may be concern about how what they do makes me look. That's not cool, right? I know! But after some soul searching, I do believe that may be part of the issue.

3. Surrender to God

In order to overcome this stronghold, we must confess and surrender our need for control. God asks us to trust him with what we can't see. Second Corinthians 5:7 tells us to "*walk by faith, not by sight.*" One article I read suggested taking a piece of paper and writing down the things that you are holding onto tightly. It then said to lay the pieces of paper on the floor and imagine you are laying them at the feet of the Father. I have done this but keep trying to pick them back up which is not what you are supposed to do! These Scriptures help when I'm struggling with surrender.

> *Walk by the Spirit and you will not gratify the desires of the flesh.* —Galatians 5:15
>
> *Trust in the Lord with all your heart, and do not lean on your understanding. In all of your ways acknowledge Him, and He will make straight your paths.* —Proverbs 3:5-6

4. Meditate on Truths About Him

Meditating on truths about God can help us to conquer our need for control. When you have a controlling thought, say

"Not my will, but yours be done!" The Scriptures shared in this chapter may be helpful to read and meditate on. Here are a few more of my favorites.

> *He says, be still and know that I am God; I will be exalted among the nations, I will be exalted in the earth.* —Psalm 46:10

> *So do not fear, for I am with you; do not be dismayed, for I am your God. I will strengthen you and help you; I will uphold you with my righteous right hand.* —Isaiah 41:10

In conclusion, we live in a fallen world with all of its disappointments, suffering, heartache, and sadness. Although we can't control this, we can be consoled because we have a God who is not only in control but works redemption in the middle of the mess.

Knowing that God has "got this" calms my anxious heart and my desire to control people and circumstances. This reassures me that all is not random and that I am not alone. So, let's clean up our need to be in control and learn to surrender to Him. Here is a final promise from Scripture to cling to:

> *Do not fear, for I have redeemed you; I have summoned you by name; you are mine. When you pass through the waters, I will be with you; and when you pass through the rivers, they will not sweep over you. When you walk through the fire, you will not be burned; the flames will not set you ablaze. For I am the Lord your God, the Holy One of Israel, your Savior…Do not be afraid, for I am with you.*
> — Isaiah 43:1-5

DISAPPOINT-MENT

UNHEALTHY MINDSETS

ANGER & BITTERNESS

PRIDE

HOT MESS MIND

CONTROL

THE 2 P'S

GUILT & SHAME

FEARSOME FOURSOME

REJECTION

WORLDLY FOCUS

Chapter Five

Purging the Two P's

(Stronghold Number Four)

People-pleasing and perfectionism are strongholds that many of us grapple with. I call them the two P's because I believe they are closely related as they are both about gaining approval from sources other than God. So, let's learn more about these mindsets.

The First P – People-Pleasing

Whatever you do work at it with all your heart, as working for the Lord, not for human masters. —Colossians 3:23

Are you a people-pleaser? Many of us have this tendency. We want others to like and approve of us because we think this validates and affirms our worth. For much of my life, I was a people-pleaser. If I did something that I felt disappointed someone else, I would ruminate over it for days, or sometimes even months. As I have evolved into a grumpy older lady, I am much less concerned about pleasing others than I used to be. Although it still upsets me when I think that I have disappointed someone or feel that they don't like me. What's not to like, right?

One of my recent revelations is that people don't think about us nearly as much as we think they do. We exert a lot of time and effort to gain the love and acceptance of other people and, oftentimes, they don't even notice or care. And frequently they aren't even thinking about us at all!

There is an old adage that I believe to be true that says, you will never please all of the people all the time. If you try, you will inevitably suffer in the process. People-pleasers believe that approval from others will fill them, confirm them, and satisfy them. People-pleasing involves accepting responsibility for the happiness of others, feeling guilty when you think of yourself instead of them, and giving in to others' desires rather than pleasing yourself.

It doesn't seem like people-pleasing would necessarily be a bad thing. Some people have even compared it with the selfless actions of Jesus Christ. The difference between Jesus' unselfish service and the actions of people-pleasers is motive. Jesus' motive was to glorify and obey God. (John 8:29) He loved and served others but was not afraid to say what needed to be said, even when it made people angry. (Mark 15:1-2)

People-pleasing isn't a new phenomenon. Let's look at some of the Biblical people-pleasers. John 12:42-43 says, *"Yet at the same time many even among the leaders believed in him. But because of the Pharisees, they would not acknowledge their faith for fear they would be put out of the synagogue, for they loved human praise more than praise from God."* The Pharisees held an elite position of power, authority, and respect. To be a Pharisee among the Jews was to be at the top of the pecking order. Nevertheless, Jesus constantly rebuked the Pharisees for being hypocritical and missing the essence of being a Christian which includes love for God and love for your neighbor.

Some of them saw the err of their ways and came to faith in Christ. However, because of appearances and the love of man's approval, they did not give up their positions. They knew that if they confessed their belief in Jesus publicly that they would be relieved of their positions in a public display of shame and ridicule. In short, they were people-pleasers who loved the approval of man more than the approval of God.

Pontius Pilate was the Roman prefect (governor) of Judaea who presided at the trial of Jesus and gave the order for his crucifixion. He was a big-time people-pleaser. He believed Jesus to be innocent but went through with crucifying him anyway because the people wanted him to. He instead released a man who had been thrown in prison for insurrection and murder and surrendered Jesus to the will of the crowd. (Luke 23)

So, what are the root causes of people-pleasing? In my opinion, it primarily comes from a place of fear – fear of rejection and fear of failure. Fear of rejection is the feeling that *"If I don't do everything I can to make this person happy they might reject me, and I will no longer be valuable."* This fear often originates from early relationships and may have resulted from feelings that love was conditional or from actual rejection by someone in your life. Many of us battle with the need for approval and the wrong thinking that, if we do good deeds, we will be deserving of love. At the cross, Jesus paid the ultimate price because he loved us. We do not need to do any virtuous deeds to earn his love.

Fear of failure is the feeling that *"If I make a mistake, I will disappoint other people and be a failure."* Fear of failure can arise from early experiences with punishment for even small mistakes, as well as having an overly critical parent or parents. Many people fear failure and are driven by the desire to be successful to gain validation.

Consider Luke 6:26:

> "*Woe to you when all men speak well of you, for that is how their ancestors treated the false prophets.*"
>
> I like the Message version's translation of this – "*There's trouble ahead when you live only for the approval of others, saying what flatters them, doing what indulges them. Popularity contests are not truth contests – look how many scoundrel preachers were approved by your ancestors! Your task is to be true, not popular.*"

In Galatians 1, the apostle Paul communicates the danger of being a people-pleaser. In verse 10, he says, "*Am I now trying to win the approval of men, or God? Or am I trying to please people? If I were still trying to please people, I would not be a servant of Christ.*" Paul was not a people-pleaser. Rather, he was a God-pleaser. He was not afraid of people, nor did he feel obligated to please them when truth or his principles were at stake.

Here is a vital truth to remember as it relates to overcoming people-pleasing: Not everyone will love you, but the One who matters will never stop loving you. God's love for us is constant - it does not waver; it does not increase or decrease; it is consistent.

The Second P – Perfectionism

Jesus looked at them and said, "With man this is impossible, but not with God, all things are possible with God. —Mark 10:27

Perfectionism is distinctly separate but closely related to people-pleasing. It is defined as *a disposition to regard anything short of perfection as unacceptable.* Perfectionism is striving to be worthy or earn love by accomplishing goals and/or avoiding failure. It may involve setting unrealistically demanding goals accompanied by the tendency to regard failure to achieve them as unacceptable and a sign of personal worthlessness. A deeply imprinted inner script convinces the perfectionist, *"Anything less than perfect is not good enough."*

Are you a perfectionist? Think about these questions. *Do you worry that you said or did the wrong thing? Expect your work to be without error? Refrain from asking for help? Read too much into others' comments? Worry that you dropped the ball? Worry about looking good to other people? Overthink things? Beat yourself up when you make a mistake or receive a correction? Are you your own worst critic?*

I thought I was over perfectionism until I processed these questions. I have made much improvement over the years but still, backslide occasionally. I used to strive for perfection in school, which later translated into striving for perfection at work on projects and tasks. Luckily, I eventually learned that things can be "good enough." I think the fact that I am also very action-oriented and motivated to get things done helped to balance this out.

My oldest daughter struggles with perfectionism and I'm pretty sure she is a Type One (the Reformer or Perfectionist) on the Enneagram. Recently, she worked on her resume for three weeks before she was ready to submit it for jobs. And action-oriented mama was about to blow her stack!

Perfectionists struggle with correction because they want to be perfect, and correction is confirmation that they aren't. However, corrective feedback is important to learning and growing and that should be viewed as a gift. We don't know what we don't know if we don't get feedback.

It's not bad to strive to be perfect, is it? It seems that it might motivate us to try to be our best. This is not accurate. We are human and will never achieve perfection so the quest for it is exhausting. If we let it, perfectionism will gradually erode our inner peace and rob us of our joy.

So, what causes perfectionism? Like people-pleasing, it comes from a place of fear. We are afraid that we may be seen with all of our faults and failures and be rejected as a result. In *The Gifts of Imperfection: Let Go of Who You Think You're Supposed to Be and Embrace Who You Are*, Brené Brown states that *"perfectionism is not about healthy striving, it is a thought process that says if I do these things perfectly, I can avoid shame, blame, and judgment."*[2] It seems silly I know. Everyone knows that we are humans and will never be perfect. However, that doesn't stop many of us from aspiring to be so.

The Bible does call us to *be "perfect as our heavenly Father is perfect."* (Matthew 5:48) The Greek word for "perfect" is telios which means brought to its end, completed, or perfect. This doesn't mean that we should be perfect in the perfectionistic sense of the work. Rather, it means that it is to be completed in Christ.

The Bible's faith heroes were imperfect. Here are five examples:

1. Abraham, a great model of faith, had his Hagar episode.
2. Moses had his disqualifying rock incident.
3. Aaron knew better but he made a golden calf for people to worship.
4. David had an affair with Bathsheba.
5. Peter denied Christ three times – even after Jesus gave him a heads up.

---

[2] Brené Brown, The Gifts of Imperfection: Let Go of Who You Think You're Supposed to Be and Embrace Who You Are (New York, New York: Simon & Schuster, 2010).

Martha, who was "worried and upset about many things," probably struggled with perfectionism as she scurried around to serve Jesus and the other guests. (Luke 10:40-41) As she prepared the dinner and set the table, she wanted everything to be perfect. She got miffed because Mary was chillin' with Jesus while she was working. The problem was that Martha was setting a higher standard for herself than Jesus was setting for her. Jesus said that Mary had chosen what was better and pointed to her example of peace and rest. (Luke 10:42) Can you imagine the pressure if you were preparing to entertain Jesus and guests? I'm pretty sure that I would have been a Martha too!

We are all imperfect but, in God's eyes, we have been perfected by virtue of being joined to Jesus by faith, which frees us from needing to earn His or anyone else's approval through perfectionism.

While we are exploring the Two P's, let's spend a little time on the tendency to overthink which I think stems from perfectionism. When we overthink, we ruminate on discussions or circumstances in our lives. In overthinking, we consider what we should have said or done. We analyze mistakes in great detail. We become consumed with *what-ifs* or *should-haves*. I used to overthink frequently. I would often over-analyze something that I said or did and think about what I could have or should have done differently. Over time, I finally realized that this was pointless and did not add value in most situations. I now see my perfectionistic daughter doing this. She often gets stuck in analysis paralysis because she is afraid to make a move for fear of disappointing someone or making a mistake.

It is important to have some insight into ourselves, our motives, our choices, our temptations, and our actions. So, a certain amount of self-evaluation can be good, but it can undoubtedly be overdone. Too much self-evaluation keeps us focused on ourselves and the things we should have done or ought to do. We dwell on our guilt, shame, and regrets when we overthink. Overthinking can also lead to depression, anxiety, and an inability to move forward.

God wants us to demonstrate the fruit of the Spirit - love, joy, peace, forbearance, kindness, goodness, faithfulness, gentleness, and self-control. (Galatians 5:22-23) I don't see anything listed that would lend itself to people-pleasing, perfectionism, or overthinking. Ultimately, these issues are due to us not seeking to live and think as Jesus did.

So, what can we do to overcome people-pleasing and perfectionism? Here are five ways to purge the two P's from your life.

1. **Recognize and redirect the need to please others and to be perfect to what pleases God**

    Try to stop worrying so much about what others think about you and do what you feel God wants you to do. I know this is easier said than done but look for urging from the Holy Spirit on what you should and should not do.

2. **Set boundaries and designate time in your schedule to nurture your relationship with God**

    Remember that you are valuable for who you are in Christ, not in other people's opinions of you or your ability to perform perfectly. It is important to take time to nurture your relationship with God and pray about your perfectionistic tendencies. Matthew 6:1 instructs us as follows: *"Be careful not to practice your righteousness in front of others to be seen by them. If you do, you will have no reward from your Father in heaven."*

3. **Try to see mistakes and failures in a positive light**

   One of the things that have helped me in my quest to overcome these issues is the understanding and acknowledgment that we all fail from time to time, and it doesn't mean that we are not worthy. It allows us to grow and to rely on God to help us.

4. **Seek and record Bible verses to remind you of God's love for you, despite your imperfections or challenges with pleasing other people**

   Have you noticed that meditating on Bible verses comes up a lot? This isn't the last time you will see this suggestion. Probably because it is really important!

5. **Be kind to yourself and set realistic goals that you can achieve**

   Instead of beating yourself up because you did not lose ten pounds in a month (probably an unrealistic goal), set more realistic expectations for yourself, and celebrate along the way as you achieve them. In this example, you might set a goal of losing a pound a week and reward yourself along the way.

Remember that Jesus never demanded that we please other people or perform perfectly. It is futile to try to do this because we will never have any kind of lasting success. He simply asked us to lay down our baggage, pick up our cross, and follow Him. Let's remind ourselves of Psalm 18:32 which says, *"It is God who arms me with strength and keeps my way secure."*

Chapter Six

Getting Rid of Guilt and Sorting Out Shame

(Stronghold Number Five)

For God did not send his Son into the world to condemn the world, but to save the world through him. —John 3:17

G uilt and shame are undoubtedly strongholds that clutter up our lives. For Christians, salvation has relinquished the need for us to feel guilty if we repent. But many of us still exert a lot of time and energy feeling guilty. So, what exactly is guilt? It is a feeling that results from a failure to do what you ought to have done - or sometimes it can be the failure to do what you THINK you should have done.

What do you feel guilty about? I remember feeling a ton of guilt when my children were growing up. I was working, and I was not spending as much time with them as I thought I should. This type of guilt is a little ridiculous. It zaps your energy and poisons your mind when there is probably little that you can do to change it. I was a single mom and had to work to help provide for my children. On the flip side, I felt guilty because I didn't think I was working enough! My children are grown now but there are still many things that I feel guilty about. Here are a few: I did not do all I should have as a mother or daughter. I should go to church more. I should be a better friend. I should be doing more to help others. The list goes on! As you can see, I "should" myself a lot.

So, where does guilt originate? Most people are conditioned to feel guilty early in life. This guilt usually comes from family, friends, teachers, or society where we are taught to feel guilty for thinking or acting in a certain way. Sometimes our guilt comes from sins that we have committed which is certainly an issue. But many of us live with a pervasive, low-level sense of guilt because we feel bad about the things we aren't doing or the things we aren't doing as well as we'd like. I feel like I have LGGD (low-grade guilt disorder) much of the time. By the way, this is not a real medical term so don't ask your therapist about it. This type of guilt isn't based on things that are necessarily wrong but on our expectations.

As was mentioned, another type of guilt occurs when we have sinned. When we sin, we should feel sorry for what we did and ask for forgiveness. Jesus has taken on our guilt on the cross. When we repent of our sins, God forgives us, and our guilt should be released.

Let's explore some examples of guilt from the Bible. In Isaiah 6:5-7, Isaiah says: *' Woe to me!' I cried. 'I am ruined! For I am a man with unclean lips, and I live among a people of unclean lips, and my eyes have seen the King, the Lord Almighty.' Then one of the seraphim flew to me with a live coal in his hand, which he had taken with tongs from the altar. With it, he touched my mouth and said, 'See, this has touched your lips; your guilt is taken away and your sin is atoned for.'* Isaiah recognized that he was unclean when he saw the Lord, but his guilt was taken away and his sin was atoned for. And then Isaiah stepped forward to do the Lord's work. He said, *"Here am I. Send me!"* (Isaiah 6:8).

Remember Joseph's brothers? They keep coming up. They should have felt a great deal of guilt for selling Joseph into slavery. Not a very brotherly thing to do! It wasn't until they were scared that they would face the consequences of what they had done that they admitted their guilt. *"Then they said to one another, 'Surely we are being punished because of our brother. We saw how distressed he was when he pleaded with us for his life, but we would not listen; that's why this distress has come on us'"* (Genesis 42:21).

Their guilt had separated them from God, their brother, Joseph, and even from their father, Jacob. Joseph repaid his brothers by forgiving and taking care of them, just as the Lord forgives and takes care of us. Romans 8:1 says there is *"no condemnation for those who are in Christ Jesus."*

At times, we may be inclined to hang on to our sins after the Lord has forgiven us. Guess who uses guilt to keep us from God? To quote the Church Lady from Saturday Night Live, *"Could it be…SATAN?!?"* He is very sneaky and uses many of these strongholds, including guilt, to manipulate us and distance us from God. After we receive forgiveness and are moving forward, Satan will try to pull us back and say, *"Where do you think you're going. Remember what you did?"* Then, those feelings of guilt and shame come flooding back. When this happens, remind yourself that this guilt isn't from God and tell Satan to take a hike!

Guilt and shame are often confused. They are intricately connected but they aren't the same thing. I guess you could say that they are kissing cousins. Guilt is usually tied to an event. A person who is feeling guilty thinks, *"I did something bad."* Shame, on the other hand, is the painful feeling that we are bad or unworthy. A person who is feeling shame thinks, *"I am bad."* It is the difference between making a mistake and believing we *are* a mistake. Feeling guilt when we sin is a godly and healthy response. We can then turn to God and seek his forgiveness. But feeling shame when we sin is a negative and potentially destructive response that compels us to run from him for fear of his disapproval and disdain.

People enslaved to shame are constantly apologizing to others for who they are. They feel like they are flawed and not good enough. They live under the fear of never measuring up, and of never pleasing others.

We start accumulating shame in childhood. The roots of shame frequently involve abuse, neglect, or significant trauma, but shame can also be rooted in less intense experiences like being bullied or told you are stupid. Unfortunately, accumulated shame does not just disappear as time passes. Unless it is addressed directly, we carry it with us. It often may seem dormant, but it will float to the surface at times and upset our lives. The good news is that anytime shame surfaces there is an opportunity to begin the healing process.

There are a few events from my past that cause me to be overcome by shame when they come to mind. Every time shame resurfaces, I remind myself that I have been forgiven and order the devil to get out of my head!

So, what can we do to get rid of guilt and sort out shame? Here are three practical steps to declutter guilt from your life.

1. If it's LGGD, get over it. It's not productive and healthy.

2. If your guilt is based on a specific sin or incident, confess your sin and repent. He will forgive you and purify you from all unrighteousness. (1 John 1:9)

3. If your guilt returns, remind yourself that your sins are forgiven!

Shame is a little more difficult to overcome but we must do so to reach our God-given potential. Here are four strategies you can use to conquer it.

1. Get beyond shame by acknowledging it and sharing your experiences with people that you trust. Their empathy and compassion will allow you to keep your feelings of shame in perspective, and they may help you formulate strategies for dealing with it.

2. Begin to cultivate self-compassion and recognize that nobody is perfect and that everybody makes mistakes. You are not alone in your pain, and you are not uniquely screwed up. Forgiving yourself is an important aspect of this self-compassion and will help to release the feelings of guilt and shame you may be experiencing because of your past. We are called to forgive others, so we should also forgive ourselves.

3. Recognize and release your feelings of shame. Be conscious of these feelings and, when they emerge, release them to God by saying, *"I am feeling shame. I release these feelings to you."*

4. Remember that Jesus suffered shame so that our shame could be taken away and his glory might be restored to us.

Isaiah 54:4 encourages us by saying, *"Do not be afraid; you will not be put to shame. Do not fear disgrace; you will not be humiliated. You will forget the shame of your youth and remember no more the reproach of your widowhood."*

So, let's get rid of guilt and sort out our shame so that we can live the lives we were meant to lead!

DISAPPOINT-
MENT

UNHEALTHY
MINDSETS

ANGER &
BITTERNESS

HOT MESS
MIND

PRIDE

REJECTION

WORLDLY
FOCUS

GUILT &
SHAME

FEARSOME
FOURSOME

Chapter Seven

Fumigating the Fearsome Foursome

(Stronghold Number Six)

The Fearsome Foursome (Fear, Anxiety, Stress, and Worry) can wreak havoc on your mind and body. I would venture to say that everyone has dealt with all four of these issues at some point. Unfortunately, experiencing fear, stress, anxiety, and worry from time to time is just part of the human experience. However, too much of the Fearsome Foursome can negatively impact our physical and mental health and keep us from the lives that God wants for us.

We will explore each of these issues in more detail along with some strategies that may help you to fumigate them from your life. As a side note, I'm having a little trouble coming up with decluttering/cleaning words. Fumigate was the best I could do!

Fumigating Fear

So do not fear, for I am with you; do not be dismayed, for I am your God. I will strengthen you and help you; I will uphold you with my righteous right hand. —Isaiah 41:10

What are your fears? Here are just a few of mine - harm coming to a loved one, rejection, debilitating illness, financial ruin, indecent exposure in public, and failure. Also, clowns, spiders, snakes, frogs, lizards, and most bugs. Oh, and Chuckie from the movie and creepy baby dolls.

Fear is defined as *a distressing emotion aroused by an impending pain, danger, evil, etc., or the illusion of such.* Did you know that we are born with only two fears? The fear of falling and the fear of loud noises. So, when do our other fears develop? Pretty darn early, I think. I remember being scared of monsters under my bed at a very young age.

Most fear is learned. Fear of things like spiders, snakes, and the dark are called natural fears. They develop at an early age, influenced by our environment and culture. For example, young children aren't automatically scared of spiders or snakes. They build on cues from their parents that indicate they should be scared of these things. I guess my daughter somehow missed out on the natural fears part as she has a pet python named Mustafa. Yikes! Other fears, outside of these natural fears, are learned over time from direct observation, transference from others, or experiences.

There are two types of fear – healthy and unhealthy. Healthy fear protects us from harm and is tied in with our "fight or flight" reflex. It also promotes reverence and respect for God. Unhealthy fear includes irrational fears which come from Satan and are designed to make us miserable and destroy our lives.

Here is a personal story related to a fear I had earlier in life. I used to be afraid of dogs. A big dog attacked me when I was little and I wasn't a fan until I reached about forty years old. My stepdaughters brought their mom's Westie to our house for the weekend. I discovered that I kind of liked him and we ended up getting a dog of our own. We now have two dogs that are my favorite "people" and have brought much joy into my life! This goes to show that facing a fear can result in the best things in life if we just push through it.

Here is another personal example. I used to be terrified to speak in front of groups or be the center of attention. My first big step towards overcoming this was teaching aerobics. This was during the leotard, leg warmer, old-school aerobics days. During my first class as the instructor, I was so nervous that I peed my pants a little… But it got easier over time, and this helped me to ease into speaking in front of groups, which is now something that I do regularly as part of my career. And I am feeling led to start doing it more as a Christian to inspire others. Pretty scary but I know I can do it with God's help! Praying out loud still terrifies me as I never feel like my prayers are very eloquent or I have the right words to share, but baby steps!

Of course, there are many Biblical examples of fear. Judges 6 shares the story of Gideon who is often considered the poster boy for fear in the Bible. When God first commanded Gideon to rescue the Israelites, he was hiding in a winepress to escape his enemies. Gideon questioned, doubted, and inquired of God in fear. He was afraid, but when he finally put his trust in God and obeyed, the Israelites were freed from oppression.

Peter, one of the most prominent disciplines in the Bible, wrestled with fear when Jesus was arrested. In Luke 22:54-62, Peter denied the Lord three times. Why? Because I am sure he was terrified. He saw Jesus being arrested and was freaking out about what might happen to him - death, imprisonment, torture – all pretty frightening things. Peter had previously told Jesus that he would never deny him. He probably meant it at the time, but the outcome was different because of his fear.

In John 14:27, Jesus said the following to his disciples when he was on the precipice of torture and death. *"Peace I leave with you; my peace I give you. I do not give to you as the world gives. Do not let your hearts be troubled and do not be afraid."* Notice he says, *"do not let your hearts be troubled"* which indicates that we have some control over our fears. Is it possible to live in freedom from fear? If we listen to Scripture, we will find that it is our choice as to how much dominion fear has over our lives. There will always be moments in life when we are afraid to give ourselves over to God, but the truth is we can trust him with our tomorrows. Obedience does not require us to be fearless, it only asks that we have the faith to follow God in challenging times.

Here are four strategies that you can employ to fumigate your fears.

1. **Name your fears**

   This can give you the awareness and strength to deal with them. When you feel fear creeping in, identify it and try to bring your brain back to the present moment. Ask yourself, "what do I know to be true right now?" Sometimes our fears feel so real, that we forget that they haven't happened (and that they may not).

2. **Do it afraid**

   It may also be helpful to take small steps and do it afraid to get past our fear. An example might be to ask for help on something small if you are afraid to ask others for help. If you are fearful of public speaking, consider leading a meeting to get your feet wet. Stop saying that you can't or won't and go after the *"I can do it because my God is able"*.

I can tell you for sure that I will not be holding a snake or a spider – or singing in public, another one of my fears. However, I like the idea of facing some of my other fears.

3. **Read God's Word**

The Bible tells us not to fear over 200 times. Here are four Bible verses that I found inspiring for overcoming fear.

I sought the Lord, and he answered me; he delivered me from all my fears. —Psalm 34:4

All your children will be taught by the Lord, and great will be their peace. In righteousness, you will be established: Tyranny will be far from you; you will have nothing to fear. Terror will be far removed; it will not come near you. —Isaiah 54:13-14

...God has said, "Never will I leave you; never will I forsake you." So we may say with confidence: "The Lord is my helper; I will not be afraid. What can mere mortals do to me?" —Hebrews 13:5-6

So do not fear, for I am with you; do not be dismayed, for I am your God. I will strengthen you and help you; I will uphold you with my righteous right hand. —Isaiah 41:10

4. **Trust God**

If we are being honest, our fear often results from not trusting God to do His job. Trusting in Him is our ultimate remedy for fear. He tells us in 1 John 4:18 that perfect love casts out fear and that He is love. *"There is no fear in love. But perfect love drives out fear because fear has to do with punishment. The one who fears is not made perfect in love."*

Here is an exercise that may help to solidify your trust in God. It is similar to the control exercise that was suggested. Try writing out a list of things that you have irrational fears about. Then present each of them to God. After you have given them all to God, rip up your sheet. If you want to be dramatic, you can burn it.

The following Scriptures are great additions to your arsenal to help strengthen your trust in God:

> *When I am afraid, I put my trust in you.* —Psalm 56:3

> *The Lord is with me; I will not be afraid. What can man do to me? The Lord is with me; he is my helper.* —Psalm 118:6-7

> *The LORD is my light and my salvation— whom shall I fear? The Lord is the stronghold of my life— of whom shall I be afraid? When the wicked advance against me to devour me, it is my enemies and my foes who will stumble and fall. Though an army besieges me, my heart will not fear; though a war breaks out against me, even then I will be confident.* —Psalm 27:1-3

Sweeping Away Stress

I keep my eyes always on the Lord. With him at my right hand, I will not be shaken. —Psalm 16:8

Stress is a feeling that people have when they are overloaded and struggling to cope with demands. These demands can be related to finances, work, relationships, children, or anything that poses a real or perceived threat to our well-being. Stress isn't always bad. It is, in fact, essential to survival and is tied in with healthy fear. The "fight-or-flight" mechanism alerts us as to when and how to respond to danger. However, if this mechanism is triggered too easily, or when there are too many stressors at one time, it can undermine a person's mental and physical health and become harmful.

We often throw around the words "stress" and "anxiety" like they are interchangeable. They are certainly related but not the same. In short, stress is your body's reaction to a trigger and is generally a short-term experience. In comparison, anxiety is a sustained mental health disorder that can be triggered by stress. Anxiety doesn't fade into the distance once the threat is mediated, whereas stress tends to fade more rapidly.

We all go through particularly stressful periods in our lives. Have you ever taken the assessment where you get a rating of your stress level based on what is going on in your life? I remember doing it when I had a ton of big changes in my life – including a new marriage, blending families, a new job, and a house under construction. My score was through the roof. Although I didn't officially take the assessment, the year 2021 was no picnic. I lost my mom, broke my foot, dealt with a pandemic, cleaned out and sold my mom's house, changed jobs, and struggled in my relationship with my daughter.

Stress is a big issue. Statistics vary by source, but I can tell you for sure that a majority of Americans are currently undergoing emotional or psychological stress. We have been experiencing just a few little things like a pandemic, political division, racial unrest, inflation, and a war. Should I go on? I think you get the picture; people are not ok!

Being able to recognize common stress symptoms can help you manage them. Stress can negatively affect your body through headaches, fatigue, lack of sleep, muscle tension or pain, upset stomach, or chest pains. It can negatively impact your emotions resulting in anxiety, restlessness, anger or feeling overwhelmed. Harmful behaviors that may result from stress include overeating or undereating, the use of drugs or alcohol, tobacco use, angry outbursts, and social withdrawal.

As you can see, stress can take a serious toll on your well-being. Most importantly, it derails your relationship with God and distracts you – which provides a perfect inroad for Satan to work in your life.

Stress is not a new thing. Many people in the Bible dealt with it. Here are five examples:

1. Daniel – Daniel was likely a tad bit stressed when he was thrown into a lion's den.
2. Esther – Esther put her life at risk to save her fellow Jews. The risk she was taking could have resulted in her execution.
3. Joseph – Joseph was sold into slavery, and later was blamed and punished for things that he did not do.
4. David – David fought the Philistine giant, Goliath, who had been threatening his people for forty days
5. **Paul** – Paul would certainly be a contender for a reward for the number of stresses in life. He would have been off the charts on the assessment I mentioned. He experienced rejection, shipwrecks, snake bites, and was thrown in jail multiple times.

One of the most effective strategies for mitigating stress is practicing mindfulness. You have probably seen the meme that says mindful or "mind full." Mine is typically the second, but practicing mindfulness certainly helps. One way to do this is to engage in deep breathing. Discovering the power of breathing about ten years ago literally changed my life. Now when I start feeling stressed out, I pause and breathe. Trust me it helps! Additional mindfulness strategies include disconnecting from the digital world; spending time in nature; practicing yoga or tai chi, and setting reminders on your phone to be mindful.

Below are eight additional practices that can help to mitigate stress:

Exercise - Exercise releases feel-good chemicals in your brain and can provide a buffer from negative reactions to stressful events. I tend to be a bit obsessive about making sure I fit exercise in, so sometimes it's a stressor for me but I don't think that's an issue for most people.

Eat well - Eating a regular, well-balanced diet will help you feel better in general. It can also help you control your moods.

Sleep – If you are like me, not getting enough sleep can put you on edge. Sufficient sleep is necessary for optimal health and can affect hormone levels, mood, and weight. Most adults need seven to eight hours of sleep to function at their best. I get "tangry" when I don't get enough sleep (the tired version of hangry). Thinking my next book might be a "hot mess" version of the Urban Dictionary.

Make time for hobbies – Set aside time each day for things you enjoy, even if it's just fifteen to twenty minutes. Read, draw, journal, garden, etc. Whatever works for you!

Practice gratitude – Our proclivity to focus on the negative has come up several times. When you feel yourself going into a negative place, take three mindful breaths and shift your thinking to something or someone you feel grateful for.

Seek community – The body of Christ is meant to strengthen us when we're weak, help us in times of need, and support us during difficult times. Stay connected with people who care about you. Ask for help if you need it!

Lighten your load – Examine what is on your plate. Too much-prolonged stress may mean it is time to lighten your load and start saying no to activities or demands that don't fit in with your priorities.

Stay close to God – Pray through stress. This requires us to focus on God and shift our attention from our earthly issues. Read and meditate on scripture and invite the Holy Spirit to work in your heart.

If I didn't practice the above habits (especially deep breathing, spending time with God, and exercising), I would be bat sh*# crazy!

Sustained or chronic stress may lead to depression in susceptible people. Depression is a mood disorder that results in a persistent feeling of sadness and a general loss of interest. It affects how you feel, think, and behave and can lead to a variety of emotional and physical problems. Those suffering from depression may have trouble doing normal day-to-day activities and sometimes may feel as if life isn't worth living. If you feel depressed, consider making an appointment to see your doctor or a counselor as soon as you can. If you are reluctant to seek treatment, talk to a friend, loved one, health care professional, or a faith leader.

The Bible provides many examples of people experiencing depression, darkness, and frustration with God. Here are a few:

- Jeremiah – *You deceived me, Lord, and I was deceived; you overpowered me and prevailed. I am ridiculed all day long; everyone mocks me.* —Jeremiah 20:7

- Elijah - *"I have had enough Lord,"* he said, *"Take away my life, I am no better than my ancestors."* —1 Kings 19:4.

- David - *I say to God, my Rock: "Why have You forgotten me?"* —Psalm 42:9

Is it okay to talk to God showing such frustration and abandonment? God is not angered by honest words, He deems them holy. God wants our relationships with Him to be authentic. His mercy reigns even in our brokenness.

The only way we can consistently and successfully deal with stress and depression is with Jesus Christ. We must believe in Him. We must trust Him and obey Him. We must remember that His ways are always best for us.

We will end this section with a few more encouraging Scriptures to refer to when you are feeling stressed.

> *"When hard pressed, I cried to the LORD; he brought me into a spacious place. The Lord is with me; I will not be afraid. What can mere mortals do to me?* (Psalm 118:5-6)."

> *"Peace I leave with you; my peace I give you. I do not give to you as the world gives. Do not let your hearts be troubled and do not be afraid* (John 14:27)."

> *"Cast your cares on the LORD and he will sustain you; he will never let the righteous be shaken* (Psalm 55:22)."

Annihilating Anxiety

Cast all your anxiety on him because he cares for you.
—1 Peter 5:7

Anxiety is an emotion characterized by feelings of tension, worried thoughts, and physical changes like increased blood pressure. Experiencing occasional anxiety is a normal part of life. However, people who suffer from excessive anxiety or anxiety disorders often have intense, frequent, and persistent anxiety and fear about everyday situations. They may also have physical symptoms such as sweating, trembling, dizziness, or a rapid heartbeat.

Chances are that you or someone you are close to struggles with anxiety. Anxiety disorders in the U.S. are the number one mental health problem (Mental Health First Aid).[3] Interestingly enough, all four of our grown kids have regular struggles with anxiety. "You're welcome" kids for putting this out there. And my husband who appears to be the most laid-back dude around has anxiety attacks from time to time and it's not pretty.

In his book, *Anxious for Nothing,*[4] Max Lucado describes anxiety as a low-grade fear. An edginess, a dread. A cold wind that won't stop howling. He says anxiety is a meteor shower of what-ifs. Further, he points out that anxiety is not a sin: it is an emotion. However, anxiety can lead to sinful behavior. If we don't watch ourselves, we may try to deal with it by drinking too much, drugs, anger, or food binges.

I have certainly experienced a fair amount of generalized anxiety from time to time during my life. I've been anxious about what-ifs such as terrorist attacks, losing my job, my kids having a wreck, and just about everything else at some point. I've even been anxious about being anxious.

I feel confident that many people in the Bible struggled with anxiety. Here are four examples:

1. Adam and Eve must have been quite anxious when they heard God calling as they hid in the garden after eating the apple. —Genesis 3:8
2. Noah likely felt anxious as he labored for years on an ark, as others likely mocked him. —Genesis 6
3. David's writings offer insight into his fragile, anxious state of heart and mind. —Psalm 139:23

---

[3] https://www.mentalhealthfirstaid.org
[4] Max Lucado, *Anxious for Nothing: Finding Calm In a Chaotic World* (Nashville, Tennessee: Thomas Nelson, Inc., 2019).

4. Mary (who was just a teenager) must have felt quite anxious thinking about the responsibility of giving birth to the Son of God. —Luke 1:29

Consider these Scriptures to learn how to combat anxiety.

Anxiety weighs down the heart, but a kind word cheers it up. — Proverbs 12:25

When anxiety was great within me, your consolation brought me joy. —Psalm 94:19

Do not be anxious about anything, but in every situation, by prayer and petition, with thanksgiving, present your requests to God. And the peace of God, which transcends all understanding, will guard your hearts and your minds in Christ Jesus. Finally, brothers, whatever is true, whatever is noble, whatever is right, whatever is pure, whatever is lovely, whatever is admirable – if anything is excellent or praiseworthy think about such things. Whatever you have learned and received or heard from me – or seen in me—put it into practice. And the God of peace will be with you. - Philippians 4:6-9

We all have patterned ways of responding to anxiety that we developed as we were growing up.

Over-functioning – This involves moving quickly to give advice, rescuing others, taking over, and micromanaging.

Under-functioning – This involves becoming less competent, inviting others to take over, becoming the focus of concern, and being labeled as irresponsible or fragile.

I tend to over-function. This knowledge helps me to understand why I react the way I do when I'm anxious and manage my response more effectively.

You can learn to manage emotional reactivity to anxiety by practicing the pause and thinking through the situation. Ask yourself, *"Do I have enough information to freak out?" "Will freaking out help in this situation?"* Keep in mind that your anxiety is highly contagious to others whom you interact with and will spread to your family, coworkers, and friends. So, managing it is important to keep everyone else calm.

If you struggle with anxiety, the intentional stress management practices which have been shared can help. I am also a strong believer that counseling can be beneficial and that there is no shame in seeking outside assistance. I have engaged in counseling to deal with several difficult circumstances in my life and it made a huge positive impact!

Have you ever thought – *"If I trusted God enough, I wouldn't be anxious."* Do not let guilt and shame get the best of you and cause anxiety about your anxiety. You are human and this is part of your humanity. Give yourself some grace when you are feeling anxious.

Dealing with anxiety isn't easy, but it keeps us aware of our need for God and his ability to work His power through our weaknesses. Second Corinthians 12:8-9 explains how God uses our weaknesses.

> *Three times I pleaded with the Lord to take it away from me. But he said to me, "My grace is sufficient for you, my power is made perfect in weakness." So now I am glad to boast about my weaknesses, so that Christ's power may rest on me. That is why, for Christ's sake, I delight in weaknesses, insults, hardships, persecutions, in difficulties. For when I am weak, then I am strong.*

If someone you love struggles with chronic anxiety, you can help by noticing, caring, and being available to help. This could involve picking up their kids, providing a meal, or lending a caring ear. A little kindness and compassion will go a long way.

Washing Away Worry

"Worry implies that we don't quite trust God is big enough, powerful enough, or loving enough to take care of what's happening in our lives." —Francis Chan

If I were a superhero, I think I might be Worry Woman. Unfortunately, this isn't nearly as cool as other female superheroes like Wonder Woman or Cat Woman. I have spent (or should I say wasted) much of my life worrying about everything including finances, my children, my job, getting old, gaining weight, global warming, the economy, and terrorism. I guess you could call me a worrywart, but I get it honest. My mother could have won an Olympic medal for worrying!

What is worry? It is *feeling uneasy or being overly concerned about a situation or problem.* With excessive worrying, your mind and body go into overdrive as you constantly focus on "what might happen." You may also suffer from high anxiety and feelings of panic or impending doom.

Worry and anxiety are often confused. They aren't the same thing but are definitely BFFs. Worry is experienced in our heads. It triggers problem-solving, creates mild emotional stress, and is typically a temporary state. Whereas anxiety is experienced in our bodies and is more diffuse. It creates more serious emotional stress and may linger longer than worry.

In a Daily Hope devotional, Rick Warren says that worrying is a futile attempt to control the uncontrollable.

> *We can't control the economy, so we worry about the economy. We can't control our children, so we worry about our children. We can't control the future, so we worry about the future. But worry never solves anything! It's stewing without doing.*

Has any good ever come from worry? I haven't seen evidence of it. Worrying wastes precious time and robs us of the ability to enjoy our lives. It's choosing to dwell on and to think about the worst-case scenario which, more than likely, will never come to pass. Worry, in essence, is the sin of distrusting the promises and the power of God. Many of us believe God can redeem us, defeat Satan, and give us eternal life, but don't think He can get us through the week. Kind of ironic, isn't it? This shows a serious lack of faith. Also, when we worry, we torment ourselves – doing Satan's job for him!

Matthew 6:25-27 teaches us about worry.

> *Therefore I tell you, do not worry about your life, what you will eat or drink; or about your body, what you will wear. Is not life more important than food, and the body more than clothes? Look at the birds of the air; they do not sow or reap or store away in barns, and yet your heavenly Father feeds them. Are you not much more valuable than they? Can any one of you by worrying add a single hour to your life?*

What else does the Bible say about worry? Let's look at Mark 13:11.

> *Whenever you are arrested and brought to trial, do not worry beforehand about what to say. Just say whatever is given you at the time, for it is not you speaking but the Holy Spirit.*

If you start to worry, it is helpful to use the Worry Decision Tree as a guideline. Here's how it works:

- Notice your worry and ask yourself, *"Can I do something about this? Is it a real problem, or is it hypothetical?"*
- If the answer is no, give it to God and move on.
- If it's a yes, develop an action plan to do what you can and then let it go.

God wants so much more for us than to walk through life full of worry and anxiety. To begin to overcome worry, we must humbly admit that we cannot do life in our strength and turn over our problems to Him. Reflect on the following:

> *Come to Me, all you who are weary and burdened, and I will give you rest. Take my yoke upon you and learn from Me, for I am gentle and humble in heart, and you will find rest for your souls. For my yoke is easy and my burden is light.* —Matthew 11:28-30

God gives us the wonderful gift of life so try to live in the full joy of the day. Try not to push yourself into the future and give up the day's joy over an anticipated tomorrow that may likely never happen.

It's probably likely that the Fearsome Foursome will appear in our lives from time to time and we may never have total freedom. But let's work to fumigate our fear, sweep away our stress, annihilate our anxiety, and wash away our worry instead of letting them rule our lives!

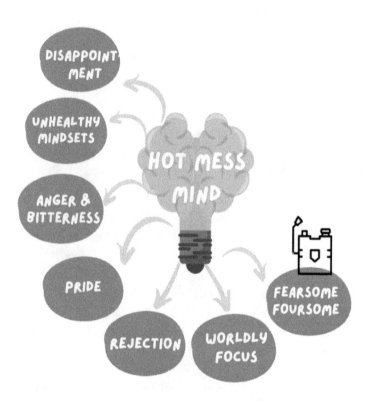

DISAPPOINT-MENT

UNHEALTHY MINDSETS

ANGER & BITTERNESS

HOT MESS MIND

PRIDE

REJECTION

WORLDLY FOCUS

FEARSOME FOURSOME

Chapter Eight

Wiping Away Our Worldly Focus

(Stronghold Number Seven)

But seek first his kingdom and his righteousness and all these things will be given to you as well. —Matthew 6:33

Many of us tend to focus on what is important in the world as opposed to what makes for success in God's eyes. So, what is success in the eyes of the world? In most cases, it seems to be career achievement, income, material possessions, and physical appearance. There is nothing wrong with these things, but it isn't how we should measure a successful life.

I have spent much of my life wanting to have more and be more. I have wanted more money and possessions; greater success in my career; and to be more attractive. But the things that the world values are not what God values. God looks at our obedience and faithfulness. He looks for humility instead of pride. In Romans 12:2, we are instructed not to *"conform to the standards of this world."*

Let's explore some of the worldly things that we sometimes put ahead of God in more detail.

Career Achievement

Many of us identify with what we do for a living and feel that this is what makes us successful in life. In fact, when we are asked about ourselves, our occupation is frequently one of the first things we share. We tend to think that if we become a CEO or a top surgeon, we will reach the pinnacle of success and happiness. I haven't seen that work. Have you? These are often the most miserable people who have become prideful and have lost their true selves in the process.

Our work shouldn't be the source of our identity, but an extension of our identity in Christ. What we do for a living doesn't make us better than others. Yes, certain occupations carry more power and prestige in our world than others. But that is not what is important to God.

I have always felt pressure to achieve success in my career. My dad is a very accomplished Radiological Physicist and probably the smartest person I know. I, on the other hand, am pretty average and inherited none of his math and science aptitude. I have felt less than at times because I haven't achieved a level of career success to even come close to comparing with his. He wrote a book about the science of dosimetry – and here I am writing about my hot mess. Mine might sell more copies though!

Wealth and Possessions

Wealth and possessions can easily numb us to our need for God and result in us overlooking the needs of others. But today's possessions will become tomorrow's load to dump. It is easy for us to want to collect cars, houses, clothes, and stuff. We have what we need but want more! I have a bit of a shoe problem. I have way more than I need but keep buying more. I have friends that are worse though. You know who you are!

We need to remember that earthly treasures are temporary while heavenly treasures are eternal. And there is something to be said for simplicity. I have been wishing for a beach house or a mountain house – or both. Many of our friends have them. But when I think about it, I have trouble keeping up with the house I have. Having more possessions sometimes creates additional, unnecessary clutter and stress in our lives. The following Scriptures teach us a lot about God's view of money which (spoiler alert) isn't very positive.

No one can serve two masters. Either you will hate the one and love the other, or you will be devoted to the one and despise the other. You cannot serve both God and money. —Matthew 6:24

Do not store up for yourselves treasures on earth, where moths and vermin destroy, and where thieves break in and steal. But store up for yourself treasures in heaven, where moths and vermin do not destroy, and where thieves do not break in and steal. For where your treasure is, there your heart will be also. —Matthew 6:19-21

Whoever trusts in their riches will fall, but the righteous will thrive like a green leaf. —Proverbs 11:28

One person pretends to be rich, yet has nothing; another pretends to be poor, yet has great wealth. —Proverbs 13:7

Appearance

Women in our society feel pressure to be beautiful. At fifty-something, I am finally kind of over it. I am just trying to get the "you look good for your age" accolades at this point. However, I have spent much of my life overly focused on how I look.

Unfortunately, we live in a superficial world where people judge others based on appearance. We would all love to say that we are not in the majority and that we look beyond what is on the outside, but virtually all of us are influenced by the appearance of others.

Who determines what a beautiful appearance is? We see images of women that represent the ideal of beauty – skinny, beautiful hair and eyes, white teeth, stylish clothes, and a thigh gap to name a few. What's up with the thigh gap thing anyway? These ideals may vary a little depending on the times and generation. After some recent travels and people-watching, I have concluded that big butts and really long eyelashes are the thing at the moment. Since I don't have either, guess I'm not part of the current *"in-crowd".*

There is some value placed on physical beauty in the Bible. Sarah, Rebekah, and Rachel are all described as beautiful. But here are a few reminders from Proverbs that godly character matters far more than beauty.

> *Like a gold ring in a pig's snout is a beautiful woman who shows no discretion.* —Proverbs 11:22
> *Charm is deceptive, and beauty is fleeting, but a woman who fears the Lord is to be praised.* —Proverbs 31:30

I can't quite get the image out of my head of a pig with a gold ring. Miss Piggy is probably the only one who could pull it off. She also has the big butt and long eyelashes thing down!

Body image is an element of our appearance that many women, in particular, struggle with. How many women have you known that have tried fad diets like the lemonade diet, the grapefruit diet, and the military diet? There was even a vision diet where you were supposed to eat everything with blue-tinted glasses. And there was a thing where you could get a staple in your ear which was supposed to curb your appetite. We'll try just about anything to get the body we want!

Genesis 1:27 tells us that God created us in His image. Isn't that amazing? We are created in the image of the most flawless, perfect being ever to exist! Our body is our temporary dwelling place while we are on this earth. Although I believe that we should be good stewards of our bodies, it does not determine our worth. God thinks we are beautiful just the way we are. Even with stretch marks. Even with muffin tops. Even with bat wings. And even with lines and wrinkles.

As we all know, outward beauty fades as we age. Although I was never close to being a ten, I'm way down on the scale now. I just saw a social media post that said, "I'm a 4.5 but at Walmart, I'm a solid 9." Maybe I should hang out at Walmart more often! As we get older, wrinkles, gray hair, sunspots, waddles, and even chin hairs (or maybe that's just me) appear. I like to think of them as battle scars. Some women resort to Botox, plastic surgery, facial treatments, liposuction – whatever it takes to maintain their outward appearance. I am currently using "bangtox" which means using bangs to cover my forehead wrinkles. Soon I will need to look like Cousin It from the Adams family.

The apostle Peter states that Christians should not be focused on outward beauty but rather on inner beauty. *"Your beauty should not come from outward adornments, such as elaborate hairstyles and the wearing of gold jewelry or fine clothes. Rather, it should be that of your inner self, the unfading beauty of a gentle and quiet spirit, which is of great worth in God's sight."* (1 Peter 3:3-4).

Idolatry

Idolatry is something that can result from too much focus on worldly things, and not enough focus on God. An idol is anything that we run to for comfort when our souls need God. Colossians 3:5 tells us not to be greedy for the good things of this life, for that is idolatry.

Back in the day, idols were often little gold statues. I have a picture in my head of something like an Academy Award with people bowing down to it. Seems silly, right? Idols are still quite prevalent but look a little different in today's world. The things we have talked about so far in this chapter can become idols. There are many other potential idols as well – children, fame, relationships, social media, sex, drugs, approval, and gluttony to name a few. Idols are not always bad things, but they make us take our eyes off God.

Surprisingly, the most common warning about sin in Scripture does not deal with lying, gossip, adultery, stealing, or murder. The most common sin that we are told to avoid, reject, and move away from is idolatry. The first of the ten commandments is, *"You shall have no other God's before me."*

Idolatry began early after Creation when Adam and Eve ate the forbidden fruit. They certainly didn't lack anything. They did it because an idol formed in their hearts, and they wanted to be like God. This was certainly an early indicator that we are people prone to idolatry.

It took only forty days from when Moses went to talk with God on Mount Sinai for the Israelites to slip into idolatry and demand that Aaron make a new God for them to worship. (Exodus 32) And this was right after they had witnessed the many miracles that freed them from Egypt. Repeatedly, the Israelites turned from God as they were distracted by riches, other customs, and different teachings. If they were so quick to turn away after witnessing things like the parting of the Red Sea, this explains why we are so quick to turn to idols as most of us haven't seen miracles like this with our own eyes. We are often driven by what we see and experience, which tends to keep us focused on the things of this world.

All too often, the biggest idol in our lives is the one that looks us right in the mirror every morning. You must admit that we are often self-centered and focused on "me, me, me." This focus on self is promoted by our culture. It is driven by the same spirit that filled the devil when he challenged God. (Isaiah 14:12-15) Here are some things that might suggest that you are guilty of self-idolatry. A few of these certainly gave me pause.

- *Do you put more trust in yourself than in God?*
- *Do your feelings matter more to you than your faith?*
- *Do you crave flattery and get upset by conviction?*
- *Do you lack compassion for others who are less fortunate?*
- *Do you use and manipulate others while at the same time wanting their admiration?*
- *Are your prayers primarily focused on your wants and needs?*

I have had a lot of idols over the years that I have prioritized over God. My kids, career, approval, and yes, myself, are things that come to mind right away. And I have a strange one, exercise. You may think, *"Exercise is good for you, how can it be an idol?"* I am overly compulsive about it, prioritizing it over spending time with God in some instances. Wealth and possessions have been idols for me as well. They can easily numb us to our need for God. It is hard for us to remember that earthly treasures are temporary whereas what God can give us is eternal.

God is jealous when we turn to idols. He wants us to be all in with Him, rather than spending our lives seeking the world's empty pleasures. He wants our time and attention.

> *For the Lord, your God is a consuming fire, a jealous God.*
> — Deuteronomy 4:24
> *They made him jealous of their foreign gods and angered him with their detestable idols.* —Deuteronomy 32:16

So, what can we do to incinerate our idols? Here are three strategies to employ.

1. **Identify your idols**

   What are your idols? You may know right off, or it may require a little thought. You can get an idea by answering the following questions:

   I need _____.

   I fear _____.

   I am preoccupied by _____.

   I take refuge in _____.

2. **Work to rid idols from your heart**

   Once you have taken the time to identify your idols, you can work to overcome them. The answer is not always to remove the object of our idolatry from our life or to stop loving it. After all, our families can become the subject of our idolatry, and the answer isn't to love them less. Our work can become an idol, but we are called to work and probably can't remove that totally from our lives as we have to provide for our families. The answer is to love God more and allow ourselves to be "filled with all His fullness" (Ephesians 3:19) so that our love for Him shoves everything else aside.

Filling our hearts and minds with Scripture will help us to be more focused on His love and glory. King Josiah is a notable example of this. When he heard the Scriptures, his heart was so moved that he laid waste to temples, idols, and any structure erected that did not honor God. (2 Kings 22-23)

3. **Pray and worship God**

Prayer and worship remind us of the glory and majesty of God and diminish our dependence on created things. We can strive to be like Habakkuk who essentially said *if I have no food, but I have God, then I will rejoice.* (Habakkuk 3:17-19) Or like Jeremiah, who said, "… *the Lord is my portion and I will wait for Him"* (Lamentations 3:24). God must occupy first place in our hearts and minds, or we will likely fall prey to idolatry in our lives.

To overcome our worldly view and any resulting idols, we should live focused on our eternal home, not the earthy one. In *The Purpose Driven Life*, Rick Warren says:

"When you believe that there is more to life than here and now, you realize that life is preparation for eternity. When you live in the light of

eternity, your values change. You place a higher premium on relationships and character instead of fame or wealth or achievements.'[5]

Here are a few more Bible verses that further emphasize this point:

Friends, this world is not your home, so don't make yourselves cozy in it. Don't indulge your ego at the expense of your soul. —1 Peter 2:11, MSG

We fix our eyes not on what is seen, but on what is unseen, since what is seen is temporary but what is unseen is eternal. —2 Corinthians 4:18

At the end of life, I don't believe that most people are concerned about their worldly possessions, the places they have traveled, their education, their appearance, or the career success they have experienced. I believe they are most concerned about their relationship with God and the people they love.

We are never completely happy in this world because we aren't supposed to be. We all have a God-shaped hole that we may try to fill with people, possessions, or power but these things will not ultimately make us happy. So, let's wipe away our worldly views and pursue the lasting joy that can be found only by knowing Jesus Christ.

---

[5] Rick Warren, *The Purpose Driven Life: What On Earth Am I Here For?* (Grand Rapids, Michigan: Zondervan, 2002).

Chapter Nine

Removing Rejection

(Stronghold Number Eight)

As you come to him, the living Stone – rejected by
humans but chosen by God and precious to him.
—1 Peter 2:4

The years 2020 and 2021 (as I am writing this) have undoubtedly been very weird. It is very strange to be out somewhere and see people wearing masks. A few years back, who would have thought that this would even be a possibility? If I had seen someone out in public wearing a mask pre-COVID, I would have been freaking out thinking there was about to be a robbery.

Recently, I rather enjoyed wearing my mask because I got carded buying wine – and I'm pretty sure that the mask contributed to that. In this case, the mask was hiding lines and wrinkles. With this and my bangtox, I looked twenty years younger! Anyhow, this got me thinking about masks and how we frequently wear imaginary masks to hide our imperfections and keep others from seeing who we truly are because we fear rejection. As discussed already, we paint pictures of wonderful, carefree, successful lives on social media. We show our fabulous vacations, our perfect kids, and our successes but most of us don't share our struggles and difficulties.

I would venture to say that all of us have had experiences where we felt rejected. Some of my personal examples include not being invited to a slumber party, not being selected for a club, having several jobs eliminated, and having a failed marriage. And let's talk about picking teams in school. Hot Mess was not too athletic and was often among the last to be picked. I don't know if picking teams is still a practice, but if any PE teachers are reading this, stop it immediately! Social media adds a whole other element as we may see pictures of friends out together (and we weren't invited) or other images/posts that result in pangs of rejection.

I know that many people have experienced much worse rejection than I could ever imagine. I regularly listen to podcasts and read books by Joyce Meyer, a Christian author, and speaker. Joyce was sexually abused by her father for many years and speaks of this often in her teaching. I can't even imagine how you rebound from that – except with God!

Rejection is hurtful but unfortunately is a part of life. In the book, *Uninvited: Living Loved When You Feel Less Than, Left Out and Lonely,* Lysa TerKeurst says:

> *Rejection isn't just an emotion we feel. It's a message that's sent to the core of who we are, causing us to believe lies about ourselves,*

> *others, and God. Rejection then can become a liability in how we think about ourselves and interact in future relationships.*[6]

The word "rejection" comes from the Latin noun rēicere, which means "to throw back." When we experience rejection, it often stops us in our tracks. It can often cause us to retreat and hesitate to put ourselves out there again because we fear MORE rejection.

Jesus was not immune to rejection. From the onset of his ministry, he was rejected by the Pharisees, the Jews, and even by his friends who said they loved him and would never leave him. With each rejection Jesus faced, he kept moving forward toward his goal. His greatest agony occurred when God turned away from him on the cross. When I think about this, I feel bad that I have struggled so much with the small amount of rejection I have faced when Jesus suffered the worst rejection ever for us.

We live in a broken world where rejection is certain to happen. In John 15:18, Jesus told his disciples to expect it. *"If the world hates you, keep in mind that it hated me first."* When we feel the sting of rejection, we should remember that Jesus never rejects us. Our self-worth should not be based on other people's opinions, but on who we are in God. Often, when we experience rejection, God may have something better for us and may even be protecting us. Psalm 37:23 is a reminder that God has our backs!

> *The Lord makes firm the steps of the one who delights in him; though he may stumble, he will not fall, for the Lord upholds him with his hand.*

---

[6] Lysa TerKeurst, *Uninvited: Living Loved When You Feel Less Than, Left Out and Lonely* (Nashville, Tennessee: Thomas Nelson, Inc., 2016).

If we don't remove the fear of rejection, we will surely be hesitant to show vulnerability. In her book, *Daring Greatly*, researcher Brené Brown defines vulnerability as *"uncertainty, risk and emotional exposure."* She argues that vulnerability is at the center of meaningful human experience and leads to courage, compassion, and connection. However, our human nature causes us to resist it. We'd rather hide our weaknesses or pretend they are not there. It's safer and we risk facing rejection or being judged by others if we make ourselves vulnerable.

If we aren't willing to be vulnerable, our relationships will be shallow and superficial. To live our best lives, we must be willing to openly acknowledge our struggles and imperfections, ask for help when we are struggling, and be our authentic selves. If we model these behaviors, others will follow, and we will develop and maintain deeper, more trusting relationships.

Young children are vulnerable – trusting, open, and accepting. They depend on others to meet their needs and take care of them. We are called to become child-like in our relationship with God and our relationships with one another. Jesus said that, unless we become like little children, we will never enter the kingdom of heaven. (Matthew 18:1-3) Further, he said that the kingdom of God belongs to the children. (Luke 18:16) This doesn't mean that we shouldn't use some common sense, but I believe that it does mean that he wants us to be vulnerable with those we discern to be trustworthy.

Christ's vulnerability has changed everything. He understands our weaknesses well, for he too faced temptation, suffering, and sin, overcoming them for us on the cross. Thus, we have the freedom in Christ to admit and confront them knowing that vulnerability neither validates nor breaks us. Second Corinthians 12:9-10 shares information regarding why our weaknesses are not a bad thing.

> *But he said to me, "My grace is sufficient for you, for my power is made perfect in weakness." Therefore, I will boast all the more gladly about my weaknesses, so that Christ's power may rest on me. That is why, for Christ's sake, I delight in weaknesses, insults, hardships, persecutions, in difficulties. For when I am weak, then I am strong."*

We are all in the middle of something in our lives. We weren't made to suffer through our journey alone. Let's be willing to get past the fear of rejection and be vulnerable so that we can help and encourage each other. It is only when we are at our most vulnerable that we can experience the connection with God and others that we were designed for as indicated below:

> *Carry each other's burdens, and in this way, you will fulfill the law of Christ.* —Galatians 6:2
>
> *The Lord makes firm the steps of the one who delights in him; though he may stumble, he will not fall, for the Lord upholds him with his hand.* —Psalm 37:23-24

Remember that God loves and accepts you despite any flaws and insecurities. Try to take your focus off rejection and focus on Jesus, your ultimate approver. Realize that feelings of rejection are only temporary, nothing lasts forever except His love. If you are experiencing rejection, he will help you through the situation and likely has something better for you as a result! So, let's try to remove the mess that rejection leaves behind and look forward to what God has in store for us.

Chapter Ten

Putting Away Pride
(Stronghold Number Nine)

Humble yourselves before the Lord and he will lift you up. —James 4:10

Pride is a *high or inordinate opinion of one's dignity, importance, merit, or superiority, whether as cherished in the mind or as displayed in conduct.* It is a state of mind or, more essentially, a condition of the heart in which a person has replaced the rule of God over his life with the rule of his own will. I never thought of myself as prideful but, as I read more about it, there have been many instances of pride in my life.

Pride has been called the "original sin" that is the root of every other sin. C.S. Lewis said that pride *"is the complete anti-God state of mind."* Pride is the root of many other sins such as:

- **Jealousy** – the resentful awareness of an advantage enjoyed by another that we feel should rightfully be ours.
- **Bitterness** – that unpleasant, lingering feeling when someone has offended us, deceived us or failed to deliver on what we think they owed us.
- **Strife** – the competitive craving to be number one including the desire for power, authority, and praise.
- **Deceitfulness** – lying or misleading others by hiding something that we think may make us look bad.
- **Hypocrisy** – pretending to be something we are not because we fear being seen and known for what we are.
- **Slander** – speaking negatively of others to make ourselves look or feel better.
- **Greed** – desiring more for ourselves than God wishes or permits.

When and how do we become prideful? Are we born that way? I don't think so but, as our fears and insecurities develop, I believe that pride starts to emerge. Pride is often driven by feelings of poor self-worth and shame. We don't feel good about ourselves so we compensate by acting like we are superior. We look for others' flaws to conceal our own, and we criticize others, so we don't have to recognize our shortcomings. And sometimes people have successes that go to their heads, and they begin to feel superior. In my work in the Human Resources field, I have seen this happen many times when people are promoted to leadership positions. They get caught up in the status and forget what is most important, the employees they are there to serve.

It was the sin of pride that transformed Lucifer, the anointed cherub of God, into Satan. The sin of pride also led Eve to eat the forbidden fruit. In Genesis 3:2-4 we read,

He said to the woman, "Did God say, 'You must not eat from any tree in the garden'?" The woman said to the serpent, "We may eat fruit from the trees in the garden, but God did say, 'You must not eat fruit from the tree that is in the middle of the garden, and you must not touch it, or you will die.'" "You will certainly not die," the serpent said to the woman. "For God knows that when you eat from it your eyes will be opened, and you will be like God, knowing good and evil."

Here are some noteworthy examples of pride from the Bible.

- King David struggled with pride when he called for an unnecessary census of Israel's warriors. He trusted more in a strong army rather than in an all-powerful God. God was displeased with the census and punished Israel because of it. (1 Chronicle 21)

- King Uzziah presumed himself worthy of priestly duties. He was unfaithful and entered the temple of the Lord to burn incense on the altar. As a result, he was cursed with leprosy. (2 Chronicles 26:16)

- King Hezekiah became extremely ill. He prayed and the Lord answered him, giving him a miraculous sign. His heart was proud, and he did not respond to God's answer, so the Lord's wrath was upon him. (2 Chronicles 32:24-25)

- King Nebuchadnezzar let his pride get in the way and took credit for building Babylon. As a result, he was driven from his kingdom. (1 Chronicle 29:11)

- Herod assumed the status of a god rather than praising the One True God. As a result, he was struck dead and eaten by worms. (Acts 12:20-23)

Maybe it isn't so great to be a King. Lots of temptation for pride to get in the way and some rather unpleasant outcomes – especially the worm one! What's the lesson here? God is quite able to humble the proud and won't hesitate to do so

What else does the Bible say about pride? Here are a few examples.

> *To fear the Lord is to hate evil; I hate pride and arrogance, evil behavior, and perverse speech.* — Proverbs 8:13
>
> *Do not keep talking so proudly or let your mouth speak such arrogance, for the Lord is a God who knows, and by him, deeds are weighed.* —1 Samuel 2:3
>
> *Pride goes before destruction, a haughty spirit before a fall.* - Proverbs 16:18
>
> *Where there is strife, there is pride, but wisdom is found in those who take advice.* —Proverbs 13:10

The Apostle John wrote about pride as the desires of the flesh, the desires of the eyes, and the pride of life in this world. He said that these desires are not from the Father but the world. (1 John 2:16)

James 4:6 says, *"God opposes the proud and gives grace to the humble."* This doesn't say that God simply ignores the proud, he works in open opposition against them! Pride provokes God to wrath and indignation. It irritates him, agitates him, and displeases him.

Now, that we have explored pride, let's examine humility which is the opposite of pride as well as the remedy for it. Humility is knowing the truth about yourself and your proper standing with God. It is accepting that you are weak and that your heart is beyond your understanding. It is acknowledging that you have a creator who knows you better than you know yourself. It is freedom from pride or arrogance. C.S. Lewis said, *"Humility is not thinking less of ourselves, but thinking of ourselves less."*

Humility is sometimes seen as a weakness, but this is a misconception. It is associated with quietness, submission, and thoughts of inadequacy but it does not mean that you should bow down or be subservient to other people. Humble people think soberly about themselves. They don't brag about their accomplishments or abilities. Rather, they acknowledge that their sufficiency is in the God of all things. (2 Corinthians 3:5) Proverbs 11:2 supports this notion,

> *"When pride comes, then comes disgrace, but with humility comes wisdom."*

The following behaviors demonstrate humility.

- Putting others first.
- Listening and seeking to understand.
- Showing gratitude.
- Seeking input and feedback from others.
- Taking responsibility and admitting mistakes.
- Showing a willingness to ask for help.
- Realizing that all things come from God.

Humility is important for all of us. In particular, I think that some people in leadership positions shy away from humility when it is in actuality one of the most important leadership traits. Think of the kings in the examples of pride I shared. Leaders may be hesitant to admit mistakes or ask for help as they think it shows weakness. But humility is critical in building trust and in acting as a servant leader – the best kind of leader in my opinion. Of course, Jesus was the epitome of a servant leader and is a great model for us to aspire to.

So, are you convinced yet that pride is an issue that you should "put away" in your life? Here are five strategies that you can employ to that end.

1. **Pray**

    Ask God to reveal and remove any pride in your heart, mind, and life.

2. **Read the Bible and do what it says**

    To hear God, you must listen to His word. Obedience brings blessing into our lives. Gratefulness and generosity keep pride at bay.

3. **Repent**

    Continually confess and repent of your sins to cultivate humility.

4. **Serve others**

    If you serve others, you can stay humble and avoid pride. It is quite difficult to serve others and be full of pride at the same time.

5. **Take your prideful thoughts captive**

    When you notice yourself thinking prideful thoughts, take them captive and redirect yourself. As a reminder; do what you are instructed to do in Philippians and think about whatever is true, noble, right, pure, lovely, admirable, excellent, or praiseworthy.

DISAPPOINT-
MENT

UNHEALTHY
MINDSETS

LUKEWARM
MESS
MIND

ANGER &
BITTERNESS

PRIDE

Chapter Eleven

Abandoning Anger and Banishing Bitterness

(Stronghold Number Twelve)

Whoever is patient has great understanding, but one who is quick-tempered displays folly. —Proverbs 14:29

Anger and bitterness can taint your life and make you a hot-headed mess. Anger is commonly defined as *a strong feeling of annoyance, displeasure, or hostility.* The Mayo Clinic says that *anger is a natural response to a perceived threat against our well-being or position.* This response causes the body to release adrenaline, muscles to tighten, and heart rate and blood pressure to increase. As humans, we are going to get angry sometimes, it's just part of life. Although feeling anger sometimes is normal, we should not cling to these feelings and act out or hold grudges.

So, what makes you angry? I occasionally get road rage. And I certainly get angry if someone is ugly to my kids or loved ones.

And certain people (won't mention names here) tend to push my buttons to the point that I lose my cool at times. I am sure none of you have had this problem, but I used to feel like I was doing everything for everyone in my family and that no one appreciated it. I would bottle it up and eventually erupt angrily on my family members. At work, I would often stuff any anger that I felt and wouldn't always address situations to resolve it. This may be why I've changed jobs a lot! Lately, I have had a three-year expiration period. I think I'm a Millennial in disguise.

The Bible teaches that uncontrolled anger is harmful, both to the person who harbors it and to those around him or her. (Proverbs 29:22) Further, the Bible says that those who continue to have "fits of anger" will not inherit God's kingdom. (Galatians 5:19-21) Remember Cain? Cain "grew hot with anger" when God rejected his sacrifice. Cain's anger then festered to the point that he murdered his brother. (Genesis 4:3-8)

James 1:19 says, "*. . . everyone should be quick to hear, slow to speak and slow to anger.*" He isn't necessarily saying that anger is wrong but is telling us not to be quick-tempered. Paul told the Ephesians pretty much the same thing: "*In your anger do not sin: Do not let the sun go down while you are still angry, and do not give the devil a foothold.*" (Ephesians 4:26-27). I can think of many times when the sun went down on my anger. I have slept on the very corner of the bed trying not to touch my husband because I was angry about something. Mostly with the first one!

Here are five methods of abandoning anger so it doesn't get the best of you.

1. **Just say no**
   When you feel yourself getting upset, immediately say "No!" to those thoughts and feelings. Instead of letting the anger control you, take some deep breaths, and say a prayer.

2. **Take a break**
   Proverbs 17:14 says, *"Starting a quarrel is like breaching a dam; so drop the matter before a dispute breaks out."* Although you should try to settle differences quickly, sometimes you may need to take a break and cool down before addressing the situation with the other person involved. In my work, I teach folks to practice the pause. I think this is an important practice to employ in any difficult situation.

3. **Get the facts**
   Proverbs 19:11 says, *"A person's wisdom yields patience; it is to one's glory to overlook an offense."* Gather all the facts and get all sides of the story before jumping to conclusions.

4. **Give others a little grace**
   Remember that almost all of us are going through difficulties in our lives. Recognize that there are probably underlying reasons that may be leading others to behave badly and cut them some slack.

5. **Pray for a peaceful mind**
   Through prayer, we can experience *"the peace of God, which transcends all understanding"* (Philippians 4:7).

Anger that is not dealt with will be transformed into bitterness. So, what exactly is bitterness? Bitterness is caused by harboring feelings of anger or pain towards others or a situation.

It involves unforgiveness and a refusal to be humble. The root of bitterness is planted when we feel that we don't get what we think we deserve, or we feel like we (or someone we love) have been mistreated.

Below are some distinctions between anger and bitterness.

- Anger can pass quickly but bitterness loiters and doesn't let go.
- Anger is about a present hurt while bitterness is about a past hurt.
- Anger is often loud while bitterness is quiet.

Maybe a friend has betrayed your trust. Maybe your spouse had an affair. Maybe someone slandered your reputation. Maybe you were sexually abused. Maybe your child was hurt by someone. These are serious circumstances that could easily cause you to become bitter over time.

Ephesians 4:31-32 says, *"Get rid of all bitterness, rage, and anger, brawling and slander, along with every form of malice. Be kind and compassionate to one another, forgiving each other, just as in Christ God forgave you."*

Hebrews 12:14-15 sheds more light on the concept. *"Make every effort to live in peace with everyone and to be holy; without holiness, no one will see the Lord. See to it that no one falls short of the grace of God and that no bitter root grows up to cause trouble and defile many."*

This verse helps us to understand the danger that lies behind bitterness. Bitterness is a root that grows quickly and causes trouble, division, and hatred. It is one of the most destructive and toxic human emotions. That is because it comes from allowing the emotions of anger and hate—and sometimes fear and jealousy—to linger in our lives.

Bitterness may start small but, over time, an offense can burn its way into our hearts creating greater and greater hurt. We replay it in our minds over and over. We tell it to others, enlisting support for our bitterness.

The world is full of people that haven't dealt with old hurts. And bitterness has a way of seeping into every area of our lives. It can end up affecting our physical and mental health as well as our relationships. Some people don't even know that they are bitter. They walk around unhappy most of the time and never stop to think why. They argue with anyone who gives them the opportunity, are overly critical, and harbor hatred in their hearts. Does this remind you of anyone you know?

Consider these Scriptures:

> *If it is possible, as far as it depends on you, live at peace with everyone.*
> —Romans 12:18
> *But I tell you, love your enemies and pray for those who persecute you.*
> —Matthew 5:44

Live at peace with everyone? Love our enemies? Pray for our persecutors? Those are tall orders. I might pray something like, *"please give that person what's coming to them"* but I don't think this is what Jesus had in mind.

How can we prevent bitterness from moving into our hearts? How can we deal with our enemies? One word – forgiveness. The Bible says:

> *"For if you forgive other people when they sin against you, your heavenly Father will also forgive you. But if you do not forgive others their sins, your Father will not forgive your sins"* (Matthew 6:14-15).

If God can forgive us for our sins, we should be able to forgive others! But what about mean girls? I can tell you that there are still a few from back in the day that I harbor some bad feelings toward and wouldn't look forward to seeing at a reunion. What about bullies and backstabbers? Most of us have encountered them at some point, when we were young and as adults in the workplace, and maybe even at church. It is especially hard for me to imagine forgiving someone who wronged or harmed me or a loved one in an extreme way, such as through sexual abuse or even death.

We have all been hurt by others and it can be difficult to get past the hurt, forgive, and move on. My mother harbored bitterness and resentment towards my dad for his actions, resulting in their divorce, for over forty years. She ended up remarrying someone with whom she was much happier, but her life was tainted by bitterness. She would often say that my dad was "dead to her." She was a little bit dark. She was also the only eighty-year-old I know of that enjoyed *Trailer Park Boys* and *It's Always Sunny in Philadelphia*. She may be – and by may be I mean definitely - part of what contributed to my hot mess!

Forgiveness is defined as a conscious, deliberate decision to release feelings of resentment or vengeance toward a person or group who has harmed you, regardless of whether they deserve your forgiveness. Forgiveness benefits us and is critical to our happiness and growth. When we hold onto hurt, pain, bitterness, and anger, it harms us much more than it does the other person. Some of the last words that Jesus uttered were *"Father, forgive them for they know not what they do."*

How many times must we forgive someone if they wrong us? Matthew 18:21-22 tells us – well sort of.

> *Peter came to Jesus and asked, "Lord, how many times should I forgive my brother when he sins against me. Up to seven times?" Jesus answered, "I tell you not seven times, but seventy- seven times.*

That's a lot of times. I think it means as many as it takes. Often, we may not feel like forgiving someone but it's important to understand that forgiveness doesn't necessarily excuse wrongdoings. It's not a pardon or condoning what the other person has done. Forgive and forget is not a biblical quote. Forgiving doesn't negate the pain or reverse things that have happened, it just frees you from the burden of hatred and bitterness. Choosing not to forgive gets us stuck in our past, preventing us from moving forward.

I know there have been times in my life when I struggled to forgive and held on to bitterness. I eventually realized that this was only really hurting me and was hindering me from having peace in my life. You have probably heard the adage that *"hurt people hurt people."* Seeing things from this perspective and understanding that unresolved hurt may be impacting others' actions has been helpful to me in forgiving others for injustices.

What can you do to banish bitterness from your life and move toward forgiveness? Here are three actions to consider.

1. **Remember that to forgive doesn't mean you have to forget**

   You are simply letting go of the past and moving forward. As long as you have unforgiveness in your heart, you will be separated from God. If God can forgive us for the bad stuff we've done, we should forgive others. Romans 3:23 says, *"For all have sinned and fall short of the glory of God."*

2. **Think of your "enemies" as fellow human beings and children of God who are loved by Him**

   You should do your best to show them respect and compassion.

3. **Pray and ask for help**

If you are having trouble letting go of bitterness and forgiving someone, pray about it and ask God to help you! You may also want to talk to a friend or spiritual counselor who may be able to help you move forward.

Chapter Twelve

Minimizing Unhealthy Mindsets

(Stronghold Number Eleven)

As we go through life, we often develop unhealthy or negative mindsets that can easily turn into strongholds. Let's examine some of these unhealthy mindsets including victim mentality, martyr complex, negativity, entitlement, and doubt.

Vacating Victim Mentality & Minimizing Martyr Complex

What, then, shall we say in response to these things? If God is for us, who can be against us?—Romans 8:31

We have all been victimized at some point in our lives. Maybe bad things happened in your childhood. You had a tough breakup. You lost your job. You suffered the loss of a loved one. Bad things happen to all of us. It is how we respond that makes a big difference.

Have you ever been guilty of having a victim mentality? This comes into play when you blame everyone else for what happens in your world. You think that the future only holds bad things for you. The deception, *"It's never my fault,"* is at the core of the victim mentality.

A victim mentality may develop in response to abuse, trauma, or betrayal. This mindset may also develop for those who are in codependent relationships where they sacrifice their goals to support someone else. Some may take on the role of the victim to manipulate others for sympathy and attention.

This may sound strange, but sometimes people get comfortable being the victim. They grow used to feeling sorry for themselves and inviting others to join them. They like having pity parties. I love a good pity party occasionally, complete with Hallmark movies and ice cream. But no one likes those who are continually playing the victim. Furthermore, it is not Christ-like behavior.

Recently, a friend made comments like, *"things never work out for me"* and *"the odds are always against me."* This shows a victim mentality. And for sure, she has been a victim - as we all have – but we must overcome the urge to see ourselves this way.

At work, I have frequently witnessed employees who show a victim mentality. Everything is someone else's fault. They deflect feedback and point fingers at other people or circumstances. If you tend to do this at work or in other areas of your life, take responsibility. Others will respect you for it. Playing the victim reflects negatively on you and doesn't demonstrate Christian values.

Too bad this book isn't a good platform for some of my other HR stories. I have entertaining ones like the person who flushed the toilet on a phone interview, the employee that robbed a bank, and there is the erotic cookie story. That one is probably R-rated. An idea for a future book – Hot Mess HR!

The Bible validates that there are victims in life. Psalm 10:14 says, *"But you, God, see the trouble of the afflicted; you consider their grief and take it in hand. The victims commit themselves to you; you are the helper of the fatherless."* This verse tells us that, if we commit ourselves to God, He will help us to overcome! God does not want those moments when you have been victimized to become a mindset that will affect everything that happens in your life. He wants us to have the mindset that we can do all things through Him.

Jesus is the ultimate example of someone who was victimized but never had a victim mentality. Can you fathom everything that he endured? They whipped him, plucked his beard, spat at him, mocked him, put a crown of thorns on his head, and hung him from the cross. And he was completely blameless. Jesus never complained about how he was treated or felt sorry for himself. First Peter 2:22-23 says, *"He committed no sin, and no deceit was found in His mouth. When they hurled their insults at him, he did not retaliate; when he suffered, he made no threats. Instead, he entrusted himself to him who judges justly."*

Joseph is another example of someone who could have easily slipped into a victim mentality. He was sold into slavery by his brothers and then falsely accused by a woman who wanted to seduce him. Later, he was forgotten by a man who promised to put in a word for him to help him get out of jail. I think I would have a chip on my shoulder after going through all of that! But he showed forgiveness, reassurance, and kindness to his brother, despite what they did to him.

We all face struggles in our lives, but we can choose our attitude in the midst of them. We can wallow in self-pity, take no responsibility, and allow a victim mentality to cast blame on everyone and everything. Or we can start taking responsibility for our lives and our actions and be a victor instead of a victim!

Whenever you feel the urge to slip into a victim mentality, declare the following Scriptures over your life.

> *But thanks be to God! He gives us victory through our Lord Jesus Christ.* —1 Corinthians 15:57)
>
> *No, in all these things we are more than conquerors through him who loved us.* —Romans 8:37
>
> *I have told you these things, so that in me you may have peace. In this world you will have trouble. But take heart! I have overcome the world.* —John 16:33

You have probably also heard the term, martyr, and may wonder how it differs from the victim. Martyr complex is similar to a victim mentality, but the two mindsets have some subtle differences. A person with a victim mentality typically feels personally victimized by anything that goes wrong, even when the problem or behavior wasn't directed at them.

Martyr complex goes beyond feeling like a victim. Martyrs go out of their way to find situations that are likely to cause them distress or suffering. They sacrifice their own needs to do things for others. That sounds like a nice thing to do, right? Well, it doesn't come from a good place in the martyr's case, they do it out of obligation or guilt and feel that they are victims of the demands of others. They are afraid that, if they aren't serving others, they don't have value. The thing is that, over time, this makes them tired and resentful. The Bible says, "*Each of you should give what you have decided in your heart to give, not reluctantly or under compulsion, for God loves a cheerful giver*" (2 Corinthians 9:7). This is not the motivation in the case of the martyr.

Remember Raymond's mother, Marie on *Everybody Loves Raymond*? Marie always wanted attention. She would do lots of things to get it and then complain that she wasn't appreciated. In the Bible, Martha was a bit of a martyr, feverishly preparing for her guests and washing dishes while feeling sorry for herself and complaining about it.

Martyrdom traditionally refers to an experience of suffering persecution, torture, and death on account of one's faith. There were many martyrs in the Bible – Able, Zechariah, John the Baptist, and Stephen to name a few. And there are certainly still people in the world that are martyrs based on their faith. However, modern-day martyrdom in the sense I'm referring to is a little different. It can result from childhood experiences or abuse. Often the behavior of the parents, particularly if they played the role of a victim, can result in the child ending up valuing self-sacrifice in relationships. A person with this complex usually has low self-esteem and looks to others to obtain validation, approval, and acceptance.

I probably had a touch of martyr complex as a young mother. I worked outside the home and took care of everything for my husband and kids. I would let my frustration build up until I was very tired and resentful. Then, I would stomp around, doing things loudly thinking my husband might notice. I felt sorry for myself and wanted to hear some words of appreciation. But thank you never came, and no one else seemed to notice my stomping around. To make things worse, I would take on other things outside of these responsibilities because I had a little problem with saying no.

Martyrdom falls into a dysfunctional pattern of interaction called the Karpman drama triangle.[7] This triangle developed by psychiatrist Stephen Karpman consists of three possible roles: victim, rescuer, and persecutor. The martyr's role in this triangle is typically the rescuer. The rescuer is the classic co-dependent,

---

[7] www.karpmandramatriangle.com

enabling, overly protective person - Ms. or Mr. "Fix It". Taking care of others is the rescuer's means of feeling worthwhile. After all, there's no better way to feel important than to be a savior. Rescuers believe in their goodness as chief caretakers and see themselves as heroes. Behind all of this is a belief that, if they take care of others, then sooner or later, others will take care of them too. When that doesn't happen, the martyr complex often emerges.

So, why do people keep operating in this mode? It is partly a matter of being in control. Martyrs think that if they don't do something, it won't get done or won't get done as well. They like to feel that they are essential and that the world depends on them. Channeling the bulk of their energy into external situations is also a distraction from dealing with their own issues.

If being a martyr is a role you've fallen into, you should consider altering the script. Lower the bar a little in your life. Of course, you want things done your way and, on your timeline, but this is going to have to change if you want out. Accept that not every task is critical and adjust your standards. Your house doesn't have to be spotless all the time. You don't have to do everything perfectly. You don't have to handle everything for everyone else. Give yourself a break.

Most people with martyr tendencies find it challenging to express their emotions and needs. Helping others might be important to you, but if you've reached your limit, there is nothing wrong with saying no. And if it makes you feel better, you can soften it with a polite explanation. You will have many opportunities to play the savior and save the day. But before you fall on your sword, check your intentions, and determine if it's something that you really should do or if it's overkill and you are slipping into that martyr role.

Scripture tells us, *"It is for freedom that Christ has set us free. Stand firm, then, and do not let yourselves be burdened again by a yoke of slavery"* (Galatians 5:1).

If you suffer from victim mentality and/or martyr complex, declutter these mindsets from your life and set yourself free. Free to be who you were meant to be in Christ!

Negating Negativity

Do not be misled: 'Bad company corrupts good character.'
—1 Corinthians 15:33

The negativity bias refers to our proclivity to listen to, learn from, and use negative information much more than positive. Negative news and information are constantly coming at us from the media and other sources. Maybe part of the reason why is that this is what we tend to focus on.

If you have ever driven by the scene of a wreck or fire, you likely noticed that people stop or slow down to check out what's happening. It seems to pique our interest if we think something bad has happened. This focus on negative information can explain why we frequently recall and think about criticism more than positive comments; dwell on unpleasant events more than pleasant ones; and focus our attention more quickly on negative rather than positive information.

I have observed this tendency in myself. I can be having a great day where almost everything is going well, and I will dwell on the one bad thing that occurred. Maybe someone sent me a snarky email or looked at me funny that day. I ruminate over that one thing over all the good things that happened.

Debbie Downer is one of my favorite characters on *Saturday Night Live*. If you aren't familiar, she is always bringing others down with random negative comments. In my favorite episode, she was with a group that was talking about how excited they were after their first day at Disneyland. Debbie inserted negative comments throughout the conversation and ended with the announcement that her cat had feline aids.

Eeyore is a fictional character in the Winnie-the-Pooh books by A. A. Milne. He is generally characterized as a negative, gloomy, old grey stuffed donkey who is a friend of Winnie-the-Pooh. He always has something negative to say to bring down Pooh, Piglet, and the rest of the gang. I'm surprised they want to hang out with Eeyore. I'm not sure I would.

We all have negative people in our lives that drain our energy and optimism. It can be exhausting. And we may even be that person from time to time! My mother always had sort of a Negative Nelly personality. I loved her very much, but she always tended to focus on the negative aspects of every situation. Maybe she was wired more that way than other people, or maybe this pattern of behavior developed throughout her life. That being the case, I have tried very hard to overcome the tendency to be negative and have a "glass half full" mentality but it is a daily struggle.

One way that we show negativity is through complaining. Since Adam and Eve were first banished from the Garden of Eden (Genesis 3:23), life has been hard, and we have been complaining about it. Unfortunately, it is in our sinful nature to focus on ourselves and to complain when our desires are not being met.

I was participating in a seven-day no complaining challenge at work. I thought this challenge would be a piece of cake, but I didn't even make it through the morning on the first day. I don't think we realize how much we do complain! I wasn't consciously aware of it until I was making a deliberate effort not to.

Talk about complaining! The Israelites were master whiners and complainers. Each time they would complain, there would be a negative consequence, but then they would pretty much immediately begin to complain again. The book of Numbers is full of grumbling, destruction, and then more complaints. A whole subheading in Chapter Eleven of Numbers was called *The People Complained.* Numbers 11:1-2 says:

> *Now the people complained about their hardships in the hearing of the Lord, and when he heard them his anger was aroused. Then fire from the Lord burned among them and consumed some of the outskirts of the camp. When the people cried out to Moses, he prayed to the Lord and the fire died down.*

The Israelites whined about the manna God gave them. They dwelled in the past and even said they wished they were still in slavery in Egypt because there, they had meat. Now I'm not a vegetarian, but I would certainly prefer no meat to slavery. Just sayin'. They grumbled about the leadership God had given them and complained that they were not strong enough to enter the land God had promised them. As a result, they ended up dying in the desert, and never got to enter the promised land.

So, how do we overcome our inclination to go negative? Here are five suggestions that may help.

1. **Develop self-awareness and challenge negative self-talk**

   By checking on yourself throughout the day, you can become more conscious of thoughts that are running through your mind – both positive and negative. You can examine your behaviors as well to better understand what is serving you well and what isn't. Once you become more self-aware, you can begin to tackle these thoughts by challenging them and replacing them with more positive thoughts. Here is a personal example. I often beat myself up if I make a mistake and tend to dwell on it. I have learned to reframe this by thinking about all the things that I did right and further by reminding myself that we all make mistakes, and they are learning opportunities.

2. **Savor the positive moments**

    As we've seen, negativity is very much where we direct our attention. By directing more of our conscious attention toward the positive events and feelings we experience, we can begin to address the asymmetry of negativity bias. The next time you have a positive moment, stay with it and enjoy it. Engage fully in the good sensations, happy thoughts, and pleasant emotions that you feel, and make a note of what you enjoyed about it.

    God desires for us to have a positive perspective and see our lives as overflowing with His love, grace, joy, and peace. When we are negative, we are not believing God's promises and are limiting our reliance on Him. First Timothy 4:12 tells us to *"set an example for the believers in speech, in conduct, in love, in faith, and purity."*

4. **Practice gratitude**

    Gratitude has come up in this book frequently which indicates that it is pretty important in dealing with many of the strongholds we experience. We are instructed to be thankful numerous times in the Psalms (Psalm 30:4; 50:14; 92:1; 95:2; 100:4; 105:1; 136:6). In 1 Thessalonians 5:16-18, Paul tells us, *"Rejoice always, pray continually, give thanks in all circumstances, for this is God's will for you in Christ Jesus."*

121

Gratitude is a simple way to overcome negativity. Research shows that when we count three or more blessings a day, we get a measurable boost in happiness that uplifts and energizes us. It is also physiologically impossible to be stressed and thankful simultaneously as two thoughts cannot occupy our minds at the same time. "*...always giving thanks to God the Father for everything, in the name of our Lord Jesus Christ*" (Ephesians 5:20).

5. **Look at what's going right rather than what's going wrong**

   Try to shift your perspective and keep your eyes and ears open for things that are going well. Instead of complaining about what others are doing wrong, focus on what they are doing right. Praise them and tell them that you appreciate them.

6. **Pray**

   Scientific research shows that daily prayer reduces stress; boosts positive energy; and promotes health and vitality. When you are faced with negative feelings, talk to God, and ask him to help you recharge.

   It is understandable when those who do not know Christ are negative because they have no hope of anything beyond this world. For unbelievers, this world is as close to heaven as it will ever be. Scary thought, right? For Christians, this world is as close to Hell as we will ever be. When we live with this focus, we are better equipped to combat the world's negativity and model the abundant life Jesus can give us.

Evacuating Entitlement

For even when we were with you, we gave you this rule: "The one who is unwilling to work shall not eat.
—2 Thessalonians 3:10

Have you ever felt like you are entitled to more in your life? A bigger house? A better car? A higher-paying job? I know that I have felt this way at times. In my career, I have been privy to salary information for employees in various organizations where I have worked. It has been hard not to have feelings like, *"I should make more money. I'm just as valuable and work harder than he/she does."*

Entitlement is the belief that we inherently deserve privileges or special treatment or that we have the right to something. We deceive ourselves into thinking we're better than we are, so we deserve better than we have. We think we deserve love, prestige, success, comfort, recognition, and wealth. We think we deserve God's mercy. We don't believe we deserve suffering, heartbreak, or discipline – and many times we don't. So, when these things occur, we grow bitter and frustrated.

The disciples wrestled with entitlement. They argued about who was the greatest among them, selfishly thinking they deserved honor and glory. Rather than scolding them, Jesus patiently reminded them of the example that he constantly set for them - serving others. In Luke 22:26, Jesus told the disciples, *"But you are not to be like that. Instead, the greatest among you should be like the youngest, and the one who rules like the one who serves."*

So, what do we deserve? The other day, I saw an image that showed a blank sheet of paper and said, "a comprehensive list of what the world owes you." This is so true! The world owes us nothing. The core of the gospel is that we are not entitled to anything, except punishment for our sins. (Romans 3:23; 6:23)

Christ is the only one who has ever been truly entitled and He certainly didn't get what He deserved.

Where does this sense of entitlement come from? When we are children in the early stages of cognitive and emotional development, it is normal for us to be egocentric or self-centered. However, as we grow, it is part of our parent's responsibility to help us to recognize that, while the self is important, it is also equally (really more) important to recognize and respect the rights of others. Sometimes entitlement can result when parents don't teach their children this important lesson.

Sometimes entitlement can emerge from feelings of being mistreated or not getting what we need. It may come from a feeling that we deserve better than what we are receiving. Finally, entitlement can manifest from pure narcissism. A narcissist feels that everything is about him or her and he/she deserves admiration and adoration. Narcissists fancy themselves as superior to others and worthy of special treatment.

In short, a sense of entitlement is the epitome of the "me" attitude where the world is supposed to revolve around an individual and what they want. As we know, this is not how life works.

Many of us have been frustrated by people who feel they deserve to have things handed over to them with very little effort. Through my work, I see this often with people who have easy availability to jobs but choose to work the system. At a former employer, an employee called in sick one day. When I went out for lunch, I saw him on the corner holding a "will work for food" sign. Apparently that was not the case! We also had an employee who had three grandmas die within the course of about three months. A little suspicious!

In general, I think we also see an entitlement attitude in the Millennial generation more than with previous generations.

Perhaps, this is because we as parents have led them to believe that they were entitled to certain things. They got the trophy, even when they didn't win. We tried to protect them from disappointments or getting hurt. This entitlement attitude of our younger generation can be challenging in the workplace. Many seem to feel that they should be promoted with little time or effort, just because...

The enemy, Lucifer, presumed that it was his right and privilege to be exalted. He is certainly not the model we want to follow.

> *How you have fallen from heaven, morning star, son of the dawn! You have been cast down to the earth, you who once laid low the nations! You said in your heart, "I will ascend to the heavens; I will raise my throne above the stars of God; I will sit enthroned on the mount of assembly, on the utmost heights of Mount Zaphon. I will ascend above the tops of the clouds; I will make myself the Highest."* (Isaiah 14:12-14).

Lucifer desired to be exalted and lifted high whereas Christ went to the grave in the greatest act of service to mankind ever. Our invitation is to serve others just as Christ did.

> *"I have been crucified with Christ and I no longer live, but Christ lives in me. This life I now live in the body, I live by faith in the Son of God, who loved me and gave himself for me"* (Galatians 2:20).

In thinking about the concept of entitlement, the story of the prodigal son comes to mind. (Luke 15:11-32) Both of the brothers in this story felt that the world owed them something. The younger brother demanded his inheritance so he could live as he pleased and quickly blew it all. The older brother showed a similar sense of entitlement in that he condemned and rejected his brother when he returned. He felt that his hard work and good behavior entitled him to be the chosen son and reap all the economic benefits. The father showed love and grace to both sons – as the Lord does to us.

Matthew 20 tells the story of a landowner. He went out early in the morning and hired workers and agreed to pay them a denarius. He hired other workers later in the day, even as late as five in the afternoon. That evening, he paid everyone a denarius as was promised when they were hired regardless of what time they began work. Needless to say, the workers who started earlier were a little disgruntled.

> … *But he answered one of them, "I am not being unfair to you. Didn't you agree to work for a denarius? Take your pay and go. I want to give the one who was hired last the same as I gave you. Don't I have the right to do what I want with my own money? Or are you envious because I am generous? So the last will be first, and the first will be last"* (Matthew 20:13-16).

In this story, the Landowner is the only one worthy to decide what the workers were entitled to. This story illustrates that God can be trusted even when it seems unfair to us.

The idea that things should just be handed to us by employers, family members, or the government is just not Biblical. The Bible clearly says that we should work hard and earn what we have. (2 Thessalonians 3:6-10) The Bible is also clear that we are all equal in God's eyes. (Galatians 3:28) He doesn't see race, sex, national origin, educational background, position, or other dimensions of diversity as making us any better or any more important than anyone else.

So, what can we do to evacuate entitlement?

1. **Own the behavior**
   Recognize the presence of entitlement and analyze why you feel that way. Think about that blank sheet of paper and remind yourself that you aren't entitled to anything.

2. **Get your eyes off yourself and focus on helping others**
   Nothing can change your attitude quicker than helping someone else. It gets your mind off of you and onto someone else and can often give you perspective on how good you have it.

3. **Understand that life is not fair**
   If you have kids, you have heard them say, *"that's not fair!"* And you likely responded that life isn't fair. Unfortunately, it often isn't. We don't get to choose our parents or lots of other things in this life. Bad things happen to good people. Find ways to make the most out of what God has given you.

Disposing of Doubt

Do you not know? Have you not heard? The Lord is the everlasting God, the Creator of the ends of the earth. He will not grow tired or weary, and his understanding no one can fathom. He gives strength to the weary and increases the power of the weak. —Isaiah 40:28-29

Do you struggle with doubt? If we are honest, probably most of us have at one time or another. We may doubt for intellectual reasons. Or maybe we are going through a difficult time and feel distant from God. Or we are frustrated by unanswered prayers. Maybe God isn't acting as we think He should. Sometimes we struggle with doubt and don't even realize it. This occurs when we try to control things or worry. This means that deep down we don't trust God to handle things for us.

When we have doubts, we can consider ourselves in good company. When Peter first walked on water and began to sink, Jesus said *"You of little faith, why did you doubt?"* (Matthew 14:31). Another illustration of doubt comes from Thomas (aka Doubting Thomas). In John 20:25, after the resurrection, Thomas said *"unless I see the nail marks in his hands and put my finger where the nails were, and put my hand into his side, I will not believe it."* Talk about doubt, he was looking for some serious validation! When Jesus appeared to Thomas, he said, *"Because you have seen me, you have believed. Blessed are those who have not seen and yet have believed"* (John 20:29).

Sometimes doubt is preceded by a period of extreme faith. In the book of Job, a massive display of faith through his devout lifestyle was a precursor to the suffering that he endured. God was so impressed with Job, he gave Satan permission to test him. In essence, although God did not inflict Job's suffering upon him, He allowed it to happen *because* of his strong faith — knowing this experience would be a true test of that faith. I do want to mention that there are other interpretations of the Book of Job but this seemed to be prevalent.

Have you ever thought that maybe God allowed you to go through some hardships to help grow you, shape you, or fulfill His plan on earth? Most Christians start the way Job did when disaster strikes: *"Naked I came from my mother's womb, and naked I will depart. The Lord gave, and the Lord has taken away; may the name of the Lord be praised"* (Job 1:21). Then, as our circumstances become increasingly difficult, doubt starts to creep in and we begin to wonder if God is taking care of us.

I mentioned earlier in the book that this past year was incredibly difficult for a variety of reasons. But I think I have grown in my faith much more than in any other period of my life. Did I have doubts during this time? Sure, I did! I had lots of moments where I wondered how He could allow such difficult things to happen to me. However, I realized that it was more important than ever to nurture my relationship with Him because I need Him, every minute every day.

Here are five things you can do to dispose of your doubt.

1. **Spend some time in nature and examine God's beautiful creation**

   Take a walk, listen to the birds sing, watch the waves, and look at the stars. Think about the miracle of birth. I believe that God is speaking of his love, power, and majesty through all he has made.

   The heavens declare the glory of God; the skies proclaim the work of his hands. —Psalm 19:1

   For since the creation of the world God's invisible qualities – his eternal power and divine nature – have been seen, being understood from what has been made, so that men are without excuse. —Romans 1:20

2. **Think about all the ways that God has worked in your life**

   Write them down in a journal and refer to them when you have feelings of doubt. For me, I think back to when I was dealing with the demise of my first marriage. I could see and feel God working every step of the way.

3. **Read the Bible and other books to strengthen your belief**

   The Case for Christ and *The Case for Faith*, both by Lee Strobel, are great reads for those struggling with faith and doubt.

These books helped me earlier in my journey when I wasn't sure what I believed.

4. **Ask God for His help**

   Pray about the feelings of doubt that you are having and ask for the strength to overcome them. Turn your doubts into questions and questions into prayers. In Mark 9:14-27, a father who brought his demon-possessed son to Jesus for healing said, *"I do believe, help me overcome my disbelief!"*

5. **Decide to believe and try to put doubts out of your head when they surface**

   There is controversy on the topic of whether we can decide to believe but I think we can. I just remind myself that, if there isn't a God, there is no hope or salvation. That is an extremely depressing thought, and I don't want to live even one day of my life with that mindset.

Is there a Heaven and a Hell? Does God exist? I'm not one hundred percent sure but I truly hope there is. And in my heart, I believe there is. We were never meant to understand everything while we are in this world. Isaiah 55:9 reminds us: *"As the heavens are higher than the earth, so are my ways higher than your ways and my thoughts than your thoughts.* First Corinthians 13:12 says, *"For now we see only a reflection as in a mirror; then we shall see face to face. Now I know in part; then I shall know fully, even as I am fully known."* Until that time, we will always have questions.

In conclusion, there are days when my faith is tested, and I wonder how there can be a God when so many terrible things happen. I still haven't figured out an answer to that question and I never will while I'm on this earth. However, I do know that I never feel alone when I pray, and I am filled with a feeling of peace. I truly believe that God is watching over me.

When you are having feelings of doubt, try to utilize some of the strategies shared to dispose of it and reignite your faith.

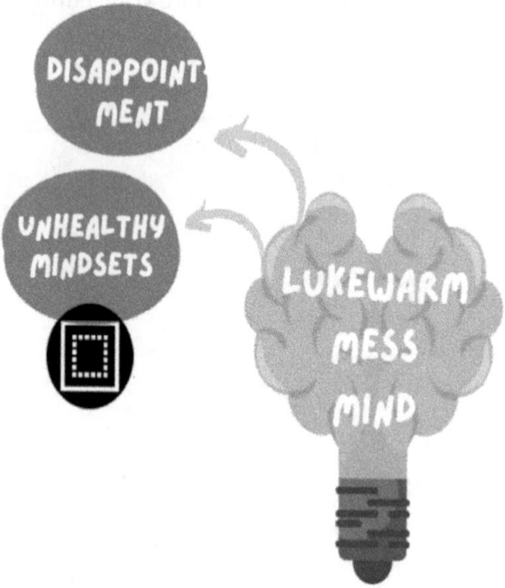
DISAPPOINT-
MENT
UNHEALTHY
MINDSETS
LUKEWARM
MESS
MIND

Chapter Thirteen

Dumping Disappointment

(Stronghold Number Twelve)

Our heavenly Father understands our disappointment, suffering, pain, fear, and doubt. He is always there to encourage our hearts and help us understand that He's sufficient for all of our needs. When I accepted this as an absolute truth in my life, I found that my worrying stopped. —Andy Stanley

Has your life turned out differently than you imagined? Do you feel that you have failed in some areas? Or that other people or circumstances have failed you? Are you disappointed that your life hasn't turned out as you had hoped?

Disappointment is defined as sadness or displeasure caused by the nonfulfillment of one's hopes or expectations. One of the things that can contribute to feelings of disappointment is a failure or perceived failure. This could include our failure, the failure of others, or the failure of our circumstances. Failure may be a strong word but basically, it involves falling short of a performance standard that we have set for ourselves or that others have set for us.

Failure and the disappointment that can result are certainly nothing new. There are many examples throughout the Bible. David failed morally by committing adultery with Bathsheba and killing her husband. (2 Samuel 11) The Psalms reveal David's painful disappointment in himself. Even after he was forgiven, the consequences impacted the rest of his life through the disintegration of his family and the temporary loss of his throne.

Imagine Moses' disappointment for not getting into the Promised Land when he hit a rock instead of following God's instructions to talk to it. (Numbers 20:10-13) Moses worked hard and was surely stressed during the forty years of wandering through the wilderness. He put up with the constant complaints and grumblings of Israel, and then, due to one loss of temper, he was stopped on the border of his ultimate destination.

In some cases, there may be someone else to blame for our disappointment. The story of Jacob comes to mind where, after Laban pulled a switcharoo with Leah, he had to work for an additional seven years for Rachel's hand in marriage. I feel sure that Jacob felt disappointed with some other emotions sprinkled in there.

Disappointment may not necessarily be based on a failure per se. It can also result when things don't go according to our plans or expectations. I had certain ideas of what my life would be like that have not come to pass. I had imagined being whisked away by Prince Charming and having a relatively trouble-free life. That certainly didn't happen as my first marriage ended in divorce. My current husband is pretty great, but he ain't Prince Charming. I thought that I would put in my time raising my kids until they left for college and then I would be home free. In reality, the young adult years has been the most difficult and stressful period of parenthood for me. And I certainly didn't expect that I would have to deal with the suicide of a loved one.

We all battle feelings of disappointment when life goes wrong or differently than we desired. Deep down, we, as Christians, are prone to the thinking that Christ should give us special treatment when it comes to struggles. We are kind of like Peter, who reminded Jesus, *"We have left everything to follow you"* (Mark 10:28).

We praise an all-powerful and loving God. But the twin truths of disappointment and an omnipotent, loving God don't seem to align at times. For example, perhaps you have an adult child that is struggling with depression and drug addiction. You hit your knees day in and day out, praying for your child....and nothing changes. You see others pray and get exactly what they ask for, delivered the next day by Amazon Prime! It is hard to understand why some of us experience deep disappointment and others don't if God loves us all equally. As I said earlier, I certainly don't have an answer to this question, and guess I never will on this side of heaven. But it's a conundrum for many of us.

When we experience disappointment, we may sometimes want to blame God. But God didn't disappoint us, life's circumstances and other people did. When something disappointing happens in our lives, it is not a time to blame God, it's a time to run to Him!

Whether we like it or not, life should be less about what we desire and more about what God desires for us. As Jesus prayed and asked God to spare Him from suffering on the cross, *"yet not my will, but yours be done."* (Luke 22:42) God is working out a plan that is bigger than us, and that will be better for us in the end.

These Scriptures tell us a little more about His plans for us:

"For my thoughts are not your thoughts, neither are your ways my ways," declares the Lord. "As the heavens are higher than the earth so are my ways higher than your ways and my thoughts than your thoughts." —Isaiah 55:8-9

"For I know the plans I have for you," says the Lord. "They are plans for good and not for disaster, to give you a future and a hope." —Jeremiah 29:11

Here are five decluttering strategies to dump disappointment:

1. **Grieve and then release your disappointment to God**

   You have experienced a loss, so you will likely need a period where you grieve the situation. Cry, exercise, read, take a trip, or whatever will make you feel better. Face your disappointment and then release it to God. Psalm 34:18 has helped me in times of sorrow and disappointment:

   The Lord is near to the brokenhearted and saves the crushed in spirit.

2. **Pray**

   Spend some time talking with God. Tell him how you are feeling and ask him to help you accept your circumstances and move forward with your life.

3. **Change the question you are asking God**

   The question to ask God when you experience disappointment isn't *"Why, Lord?"* but rather, *"What now, Lord?"* This can be a hard lesson to learn but your life will begin to change when you alter the narrative. You will likely still feel angry or disheartened by disappointments, but you'll also discover that God is eager to show you what he wants you to do next.

Not only that, but he will equip you with everything you need to do it.

4. **Assess and adjust your expectations.**
Assess your situation and then try to readjust your expectations regarding the things you want in life. Place your hope in God and ask Him to help you manage your expectations.

5. **Don't wallow in your disappointment.**
Instead of wallowing in your disappointment, do something. Help others, take up a new hobby, and volunteer. If one dream dies, pick up another, and keep moving forward. If you don't, you will likely get mired in this stronghold and won't be able to progress in a positive direction in your life.

In her book, *It's Not Supposed to Be This Way*, Lysa TerKeurst says: *"Sometimes to get your life back, you have to face the death of what you thought your life would look like."*[8] Lysa explains in her book that the human heart was created in the context of perfection in the Garden of Eden. We certainly don't live there now. We live in a broken world where we aren't promised everything we want. God knows what is best for us and He will deliver us. Let's dump disappointment and move on to live an unencumbered life!

---

[8] Lysa TerKeurst, *It's Not Supposed to Be This Way: Finding Unexpected Strength When Disappointments Leave You Shattered* (Nashville, Tennessee: Thomas Nelson, Inc., 2018)

Chapter Fourteen

Growing the Fruit of the Spirit

The Spirit-fueled development of Christ-like character is liberating, because it brings us close to being the people we were designed to be, the people our Spirit-renewed hearts want us to be. —Tim Keller

While we are decluttering the issues that hold us back, there are some natural byproducts of a life surrendered to God that we should "put on." In Galatians 5:22-23, Paul lists nine specific behaviors – love, joy, peace, forbearance, kindness, goodness, faithfulness, gentleness, and self-control – that are the result of the work of the Holy Spirit in a Christian's life. He refers to these behaviors as the fruit of the Spirit. A commentary I read suggests that "fruit" in this case means "deed, action, or result."

When a person gives his/her life to Jesus, the fruit of the Spirit is planted inside him/her in seed form. The seeds of the fruit need time to grow, just as physical fruit does. And we must constantly work to rid our lives of the "weeds" (strongholds) and surrender our flesh each day.

Here are the nine parts of the fruit.

1. **Love**

   Biblical love is a choice, not a feeling. It deliberately expresses itself in loving ways. Through it, we choose to set aside our preferences and desires and put others' needs before our own.

   "As the Father has loved me, so have I loved you. Now remain in my love. If you keep my commands, you will remain in my love, just as I have kept my Father's commands and remain in his love. I have told you this so that my joy may be in you and that your joy may be complete" (John 15:9-11).

2. **Joy**

   Joy is a deep and enduring state of our soul. No circumstance, event, or human can steal the joy of the Lord from us because it is established in our spiritual, eternal circumstances. Joy is delighting in God and choosing to rejoice and be content in all things.

   "Consider it pure joy, my brothers and sisters, whenever you face trials of many kinds because you know that the testing of your faith produces perseverance" (James 1:2).

3. **Peace**

   Peace is a deep confidence that God is who He is, and He will do what He says He will do. The world surely doesn't offer much peace. Thankfully, we can have peace in our Creator. For those who have the Spirit of peace within them, the peace of Christ is possible, regardless of their circumstances. (John 14:27)

"Do not be anxious about anything, but in every situation, by prayer and petition, with thanksgiving, present your requests to God. And the peace of God, which transcends all understanding, will guard your hearts and your minds in Christ Jesus" (Philippians 4:6-7).

4. **Forbearance**

Forbearance involves exhibiting calmness and patience amid stressful situations. Patient people don't become easily annoyed or agitated and can put up with circumstances and other people, even when severely tried. We don't see much forbearance in our world today. Everything is instantaneous and we have a want-it-now culture. But as Christians, we are equipped to show forbearance because we have the Holy Spirit living in us.

"Be completely humble and gentle; be patient, bearing with one another in love" (Ephesians 4:2).

5. **Kindness**

Kindness is being genuinely kind to anyone and everyone, regardless of differences, viewpoints, or culture. Kindness looks out for the well-being of others and shows compassion.

"Or do you show contempt for the riches of his kindness, forbearance, and patience, not realizing that God's kindness is intended to lead you to repentance?" (Romans 2:4).

6. **Goodness**

Goodness is truly desiring to help other people. A "good" person possesses moral integrity and shows it in the way he/she acts toward others.

> *"With this in mind, we constantly pray for you, that our God may make you worthy of his calling, and that by his power he may bring to fruition your every desire for goodness and your every deed prompted by faith"* (2 Thessalonians 1:11).

7. Faithfulness

To be faithful is to be dependable in our relationship with God and other people. Being faithful involves choosing to be true to our word and following through on our promises.

> *"His master replied, 'Well done, good and faithful servant! You have been faithful with a few things; I will put you in charge of many things. Come and share your master's happiness!'"* (Matthew 25:21).

8. Gentleness

Through gentleness, we allow God to deal with others instead of taking matters into our own hands. If we are gentle, we are quick to listen and slow to speak. It involves being calm, serene, and tranquil. Gentleness isn't weakness, instead, it is described as strength under control.

> *"Let your gentleness be evident to all. The Lord is near"* (Philippians 4:5).

9. Self-Control

Self-control involves being able to keep yourself in check. People who demonstrate self-control exhibit moderation, temperance, and discipline. Self-control gives us the power to say *"no"* to our flesh and *"yes"* to the Spirit.

"So I say, walk by the Spirit, and you will not gratify the desires of the flesh. For the flesh desires what is contrary to the Spirit, and the Spirit what is contrary to the flesh. The conflict with each other so that you are not to do whatever you want" (Galatians 5:16).

As Christians, we may try to exert effort to show the fruit in our lives by focusing on living out one fruit at a time. Or we may feel like we must earn it by going to church regularly or volunteering. It doesn't work like that. When we fully submit to God and allow Him to transform us, the fruit will simply appear in our lives. We will put others before ourselves. We will be joyful, even in difficult circumstances. We will experience more peace in our lives. We will be gentler and kinder. We will be more patient as we deal with situations and people. We will be more faithful in our relationships with God and others. We will exercise more self-control. As we declutter the strongholds that we have accumulated and give the Spirit more control over our lives, we will be changed from the inside out.

I know we just decluttered a bunch of stuff, but there is one more thing that we need to put on, the Armor of God. As we have seen Satan is always trying to get up in our minds and our bizness. He is not going to stop trying as he is a persistent "little devil." We need to put on the armor of God every single day to protect ourselves. Let's take a look at Ephesians 6:10-18 to learn more about this armor.

Finally, be strong in the Lord and his mighty power. Put on the full armor of God, so that you can take your stand against the devil's schemes. For our struggle is not against flesh and blood, but against the rulers, against the authorities, against the powers of this dark world, and the spiritual forces of evil in the heavenly realms. Therefore put on the full armor of God, so that when the day of evil comes, you may be able to stand your ground, and after you have done everything, to stand. Stand firm then, with the belt of truth buckled around your waist, with the breastplate of righteousness in place, and with your feet fitted with the readiness that comes from the gospel of peace. In addition to all this, take up the shield of faith, with which you can extinguish all the flaming arrows of the evil one. Take the helmet of salvation and the sword of the Spirit, which is the word of God. And pray in the Spirit on all occasions with all kinds of prayers and requests. With this in mind, be alert and always keep on praying for all the Lord's people.

The armor doesn't sound all that comfortable or fashionable but can't be worse than Spanx and pantyhose. And bras for that matter. Sometimes they feel about as comfortable as I imagine a breastplate would likely be. Nevertheless, we must put on our armor every single day. We probably should consider wearing armor pajamas too as we always need God's protection!

Anyhow, let's unpack this and look at the different elements of the armor of God.

- **The belt of truth** – The truths of the Scripture
- **The breastplate of righteousness** – Covers the heart and shields the other vital organs
- **The shoes of the gospel** – Keeps our feet anchored and standing firm when Satan tries to trip us up
- **The shield of faith** – Protects us from the attacks of the evil one
- **The helmet of salvation** – The knowledge that we, as believers, have been rescued from our own wickedness
- **The sword of the Spirit** – The Word of God is the sword of the Spirit and our greatest spiritual weapon

So, let's stand against the enemy by putting on our armor every day and keep our strongholds "decluttered" so that we can experience God's best for our lives!

Conclusion

As I mentioned in the introduction, my goal in writing this book is:

H – Helping

O – Others

T – To

M – Make

E – Every

S – Stronghold

S – Scarce

I hope that it has helped you to identify some of the strongholds that are negatively impacting your life and begin the hard work to overcome them. I think I have moved from *"hot mess to a little more progress"* through writing it. Maybe when I complete the hot mess trilogy, I will be cured.

Living an unencumbered life is going to take time, effort, prayer, and a lot of surrender! So, Marie Kondo the strongholds that you have in your life. If it doesn't bring you joy, get rid of it. I wish it was that easy, but I am hoping that you learned some things while reading this book that will help you to transition from hot (or warm or whatever you are) mess to God's best for your life.

About Kharis Publishing:

Kharis Publishing, an imprint of Kharis Media LLC, is a leading Christian and inspirational book publisher based in Aurora, Chicago metropolitan area, Illinois. Kharis' dual mission is to give voice to under-represented writers (including women and first-time authors) and equip orphans in developing countries with literacy tools. That is why, for each book sold, the publisher channels some of the proceeds into providing books and computers for orphanages in developing countries, so that these kids may learn to read, dream, and grow. For a limited time, Kharis Publishing is accepting unsolicited queries for nonfiction (Christian, self-help, memoirs, business, health, and wellness) from qualified leaders, professionals, pastors, and ministers. Learn more at: About Us - Kharis Publishing - Accepting Manuscript